TIMELINES IN SCIENCE

THE DIGITAL AGE

Craig Boutland

ROSEN PUBLISHING

Published in 2025 by The Rosen Publishing Group, Inc.
2544 Clinton Street, Buffalo, NY 14224

Copyright © 2024 by Brown Bear Books Ltd

Portions of this work were originally authored by Charlie Samuels and published as *The Digital Age*. All new material in this edition was authored by Craig Boutland.

PICTURE CREDITS
t=top, b=bottom, l=left, r=right, c=center

Front Cover: Shutterstock: Billion Photos tc, Gorodenkoff main, HKO tl, IM Imagery tr.
Inside: iStock: BrandX Picctures 7t, Delamo Foto 11, erzetic 16, infospeed 33b, Kovalvs 13, KTSimage 35, mskowronski 14, Ben Phillips 8, Kathryn Thomas 41; Library of Congress: 47; NASA Images: GRIN 5, 26, 29t, 29b, Johnson/Apollo Gallery 22, 23, JPL-Caltech 49, JPL-Caltech/MSSS, 46, 48, NASA on the Commons@Flickr 25t, Paolo Nespoli 27; Public Domain: Museum of Science, Boston 9, Princeton University 58, Thinkstock/Photos.com 7b; RoyaltyFree: Thinkstock/Comstock 10, 17t, Hemera 19, Valueline/Dick Luria 21t; Science Photo Library: Corning Inc/ Emilio Segre Visual Archives/ American Institute of Physics 15; Shutterstock: APCChanel 61, Guillio Benzin 59, Ferenc Cegledi 42, fizkes 54, fonzales 30, Galaxy Photo 33t, Grand Aquarius 18, IM Imagery 50, Chokniti Khongchum 6, Kletr 53, Maram 44, Mentor57 31, Pangfolio.com 38, Purple xsu 6, RichartPhotos 52, Rido 57, Slatan 45, Richard Waters 39, Drazen Zigic 55, zstock 56; Topfoto: 37, PA Photos 34.

All other artwork and illustrations Brown Bear Books Ltd

All rights reserved. No part of this book may be reproduced in any form without permission in writing from the publisher, except by a reviewer.

Cataloging-in-Publication Data

Names: Boutland, Craig.
Title: The digital age / Craig Boutland.
Description: Buffalo, NY : Rosen Young Adult, 2025. | Series: Timelines in science | Includes glossary and index.
Identifiers: ISBN 9781499477825 (pbk.) | ISBN 9781499477832 (library bound) | ISBN 9781499477849 (ebook)
Subjects: LCSH: Inventions–History–20th century–Juvenile literature. | Discoveries in science–History–20th century–Juvenile literature. | Technological innovations–History–20th century–Juvenile literature. | Inventions–History–21st century–Juvenile literature. | Discoveries in science–History–21st century–Juvenile literature. | Technological innovations–History–21st century–Juvenile literature.
Classification: LCC T20.B68 2025 | DDC 609.04–dc23

Manufactured in the United States of America

CPSIA Compliance Information: Batch #CSRYA25.
For further information, contact Rosen Publishing at 1-800-237-9932.

Find us on

CONTENTS

Introduction

The second half of the 20th century and the start of the 21st century have seen science advance rapidly, with breakthroughs happening faster than would have seemed possible in previous centuries.

A consumer revolution meant that more people wanted to buy more products, encouraging commercial development. Educational institutions funded medical research that could benefit public health, including a better understanding of genetics and how they might be manipulated to improve medicine.

Science and Politics

After World War II (1939–1945), the advance of science became caught up in the Cold War, the ideological standoff between the capitalist United States and the communist Soviet Union. One result was the space race, in which the United States traveled to the moon as a demonstration of its technological superiority. More recently, the challenge has become how to send people to Mars, our closest planetary neighbor. Computers were first used as calculating machines, but the type of data they handled broadened, and the speed at which they operated grew faster. The internet linked all of the world's computers and made the spread of knowledge global. Developments in computer technology include robotics and artificial intelligence. Global collaboration, between scientists from different disciplines, was crucial when the world faced the challenge of the COVID-19 pandemic.

About This Book

This book uses timelines to describe scientific and technological advances from around 1950 to about 2023. A continuous timeline of the period runs along the bottom of all the pages. Entries are color-coded to indicate the fields of science to which they belong. Each chapter also has its own subject-specific timeline running vertically down the edge of the page.

The space shuttle waits on its launch pad in Florida. The shuttle was the first reusable spacecraft. Among its missions from 1981 to 2010 were voyages to supply the International Space Station.

The First Computers

A computer is an electronic machine that handles its data in the form of digits, or numbers, expressed in binary notation, 1 and 0.

The difference engine designed by Charles Babbage was built after his death and found to work as he planned.

TIMELINE
1950–1951

KEY:
- Biology and Medicine
- Engineering and Invention
- Astronomy and Math
- Chemistry and Physics

1950 English mathematician Alan Turing proposes a test to determine whether a computer has real intelligence (can "think").

1950 English physicians establish a link between tobacco smoking and lung cancer.

1950

1950 Dutch astronomer Jan Oort suggests the existence of the Oort cloud, which extends into space around the solar system; it is home to all long-period comets.

1950 U.S. physicist James Rainwater proposes a new model of the atomic nucleus, whose shape is not perfectly spherical but is distorted.

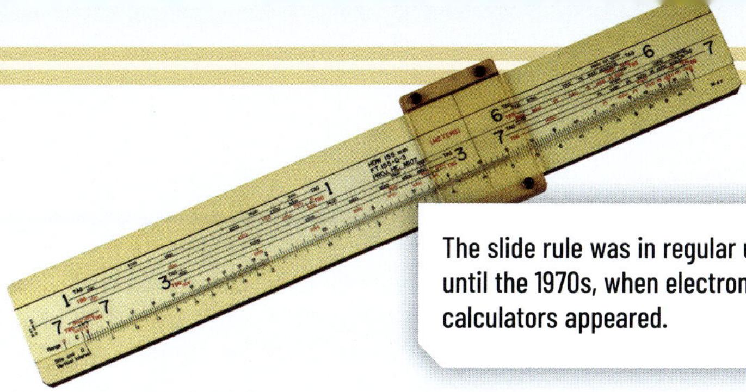

The slide rule was in regular use until the 1970s, when electronic calculators appeared.

Timeline

1833 Babbage's "analytical engine"

1890 Hollerith punched cards

1942 Electronic calculator

1946 ENIAC and Neumann's stored-program computer

1951 First mass-produced computer (UNIVAC I)

Binary is a number system that uses only two digits, 1 and 0, represented in the computer's activities and memory as on and off pulses of electric current. The first computers were used by the U.S. Army and Navy toward the end of World War II. These massive vacuum-tube machines were developed from the electronic calculating machines of the late 1930s, which in turn were derived from earlier mechanical calculating machines.

The first calculator was the abacus, a frame with beads that was invented in about 3000 BCE, and is still used in parts of China and Japan. The task of multiplication is simplified by logarithms, invented in 1614 by Scottish mathematician John Napier and "mechanized" in the slide rule designed in 1622 by English mathematician William Oughtred.

Blaise Pascal, inventor of the adding machine, also experimented with the mercury barometer.

Prototype Computers

French scientist Blaise Pascal probably invented the first mechanical adding machine in 1642. It had a

1951 U.S. researchers at the Eastman Kodak Company discover what will become known as "superglue."

1951 U.S. computer pioneers John Mauchly and John Eckert build UNIVAC 1, the first commercial computer in the United States.

1951

1951 U.S. chemist Linus Pauling discovers the spiral structure of some proteins.

1951 U.S. astronomer William Morgan provides evidence that our galaxy (the Milky Way) is a typical spiral galaxy.

Jacquard's First "Programs"

French weaver Joseph Jacquard invented the first "programs" long before computers existed. Jacquard designed a textile loom that he programmed with a sequence of cards with lines of holes punched in them. Each line on the card corresponded to a line in the cloth. Each hole dictated whether one of the hooks on the loom head was up or down. The hooks carried thread that was therefore either present or absent from the woven cloth, creating the colored pattern.

system of intermeshed cogs, a method also adopted by English mathematician Charles Babbage in his "analytical engine" of 1833. This machine could be programmed for a particular calculation and was therefore a computer (but not electronic). From the 1880s, inventors such as the American William Burroughs developed calculating machines with keyboards. Later versions also provided a printout of the results.

Early methods of feeding data into programmable machines mainly used punched tape or punched cards. Around 1805, Joseph Jacquard designed a loom that could weave various patterns in carpets by following instructions on an endless belt of punched cards. American inventor Herman Hollerith used similar cards to record and analyze results of the 1890 U.S. census. The company that Hollerith formed later became part of International Business Machines (IBM).

Punch cards were used for programming on early computers.

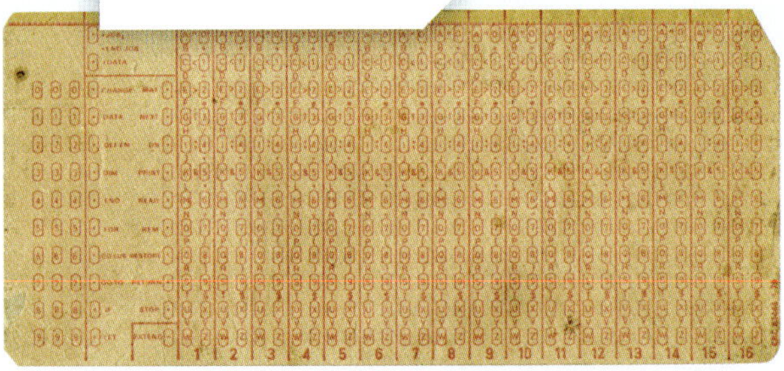

Entrance of Electronics

Electromechanical calculators appeared in the 1930s, invented by American scientists such as Vannevar Bush and

TIMELINE

1952–1953

KEY:

- Biology and Medicine
- Engineering and Invention
- Chemistry and Physics

1952 U.S. physician Jonas Salk develops a vaccine against polio.

1952 A De Havilland Comet makes the first scheduled flight by a jet airliner (from London to Johannesburg).

1952

1952 U.S. government scientists explode the first hydrogen bomb.

1952 U.S. mathematician Grace Hopper writes a compiler computer program, A-0.

John Atanasoff. By 1942, Atanasoff had constructed an electronic calculator (the ABC) using vacuum tubes that could be programmed for processing data, arguably the first true computer. At Harvard in 1944, Howard Aiken had a manually operated digital machine controlled by punched paper tape, and in 1946, the all-electronic ENIAC (Electronic Numerical Integrator and Calculator) computer was in use, although it still employed vacuum tubes.

This is the control panel of a UNIVAC 1 computer. The UNIVAC 1 was used to tabulate the results of the 1954 U.S. census.

At Princeton in 1946, mathematician John von Neumann built the first machine with a stored program that used binary numbers. The idea was incorporated into UNIVAC 1, the first computer to be manufactured in quantity in the United States in 1951. In 1949, a team at Manchester University, England, built a machine with a stored program under Alan Turing, who had worked at Princeton. The Manchester machine was so successful that the British government had it manufactured. Eight of the Mark 1 computers were sold, which was a large number at the time.

After the invention of the transistor in the late 1940s, computers became faster and smaller. By the 1960s, silicon chips arrived, enabling circuits designed in 1970 to incorporate a complete computer microprocessor on a single chip. Microchips are used in personal computers (PCs), domestic appliances, automobiles, and industrial robots.

1953 Soviet scientists test their first hydrogen bomb.

1953 Biophysicists Francis Crick, Maurice Wilkins, and James Watson, supported by the work of physical chemist Rosalind Franklin, determine the structure of the DNA molecule.

1953

1953 English engineer Christopher Cockerell begins to develop the hovercraft.

1953 U.S. surgeon John Gibbo Jr. performs the first successful open-heart surgery on a human patient.

DNA: The Double Helix

Before the 1950s, scientists already knew genes carried on chromosomes were the units of inheritance. These chromosomes are a mixture of proteins and DNA.

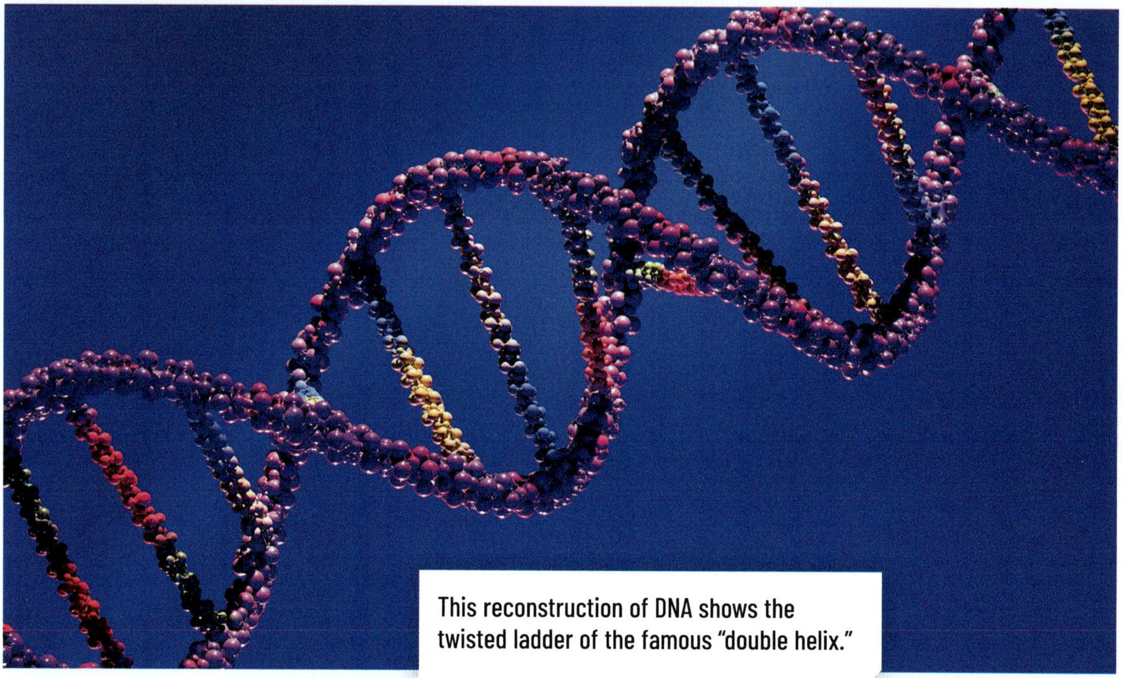

This reconstruction of DNA shows the twisted ladder of the famous "double helix."

TIMELINE
1954–1956

KEY:

Biology and Medicine

Engineering and Invention

Chemistry and Physics

1954 A successful field test of Jonas Salk's polio vaccine is held in the United States.

1954 U.S. electronics engineer Gordon Teal develops the silicon transistor.

1954

1954 U.S. truck operator Malcolm MacLean introduces standard-sized transportation containers.

1954 French inventor Marc Grégoire invents the nonstick cooking pan.

In 1951, American Linus Pauling described a class of proteins in which the molecules took the form of a helix (a three-dimensional spiral). He then looked at DNA (deoxyribonucleic acid).

Watson and Crick

For Francis Crick at Cambridge, England, the structure of DNA was an obsession. He and American James Watson began working on it. Their work was kept low key. Competition between the great research institutions was frowned upon, and deciphering the structure of DNA was also the aim of scientists at Kings College, London. There, Maurice Wilkins and Rosalind Franklin were doing a series of experiments using X-ray diffraction to find DNA's structure.

Timeline

1951 Helical proteins

1952 Pauling model

1953 Watson and Crick papers describing the double helix structure of DNA

1973 First genetically engineered organism

1982 Genetically engineered insulin

DNA explains why some twins are identical.

1955 Indian scientist Narinder Kapany develops optical fibers for carrying light over long distances.

1955 Bell Laboratories builds the first computer using transistors instead of vacuum tubes.

1956 U.S. physicists Clyde Cowan and Frederick Reines discover the neutrino, a subatomic particle.

1955

1956

1955 Scientists at General Electric produce small synthetic diamonds from graphite.

1955 The British company Rolls Royce develops an experimental vertical take-off and landing (VTOL) aircraft.

1956 The company Ampex markets a videotape recorder, designed by U.S. electronics engineer Alexander Poniatoff.

Secret of Replication

When the strands of the double helix separate, the bases that link the strands are exposed. Spare nucleotides are drawn to the two unzipped strands and link up to form new strands. The bases always pair up in the same way (A to T and G to C), so they produce two double helices identical to the original. Rarely, something goes wrong with the copying process, and a mutation takes place, meaning that one of the new strands differs from the original.

In 1951, Watson and Crick produced a model of DNA as a triple helix. Franklin disagreed, as the structure did not conform to her data. Watson and Crick started again. In 1952, Linus Pauling presented his model, but he had also got it wrong.

DNA contains four different chemical compounds (bases): adenine (A), cytosine (C), guanine (G), and thymine (T). The realization that they paired off in a predictable way set Watson and Crick on the right track.

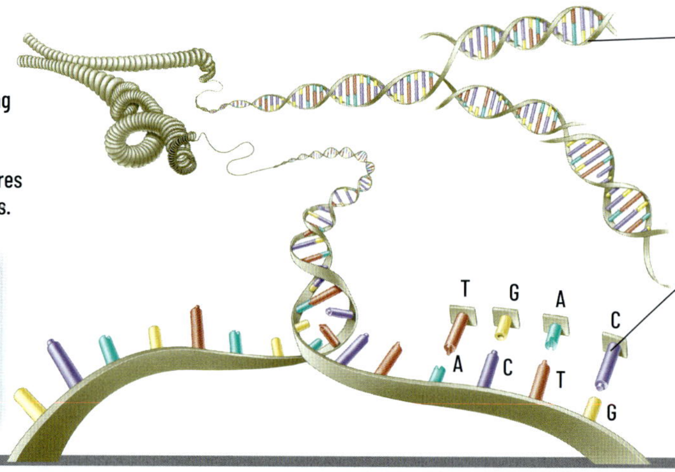

TIMELINE
1956–1958

KEY:
- Biology and Medicine
- Engineering and Invention
- Astronomy and Math

1956 U.S. computer programmers at IBM devise the FORTRAN computer language.

1956 U.S. physician Edward Thomas carries out the first successful bone marrow transplant operation.

1957 U.S. physicist Eugene Parker discovers the solar wind, streams of particles ejected from the sun.

1957 Commercial production of polypropene plastic begins in Italy.

Genetic Engineering

By the early 1950s, a number of discoveries took place concerning bacterial plasmids, which are tiny circlets of DNA that are easily isolated and manipulated and can be reinserted into cells in a modified form. They provided one of modern genetics' most important tools.

In 1968, Stewart Linn and Werner Arber discovered restriction enzymes that "cut" DNA in certain places. The cut ends bind back together or splice with the ends of other sections of DNA. In 1969, Jonathan Beckwith isolated a single gene. This made it possible to delete or insert new genes into a sequence of DNA. In 1973, Stanley Cohen and Herbert Boyer removed a section of DNA and replaced it with a gene from a different bacterium. This was the first genetically engineered organism.

Genetic engineering has allowed the development of new strands of food crops.

Genetic engineering allows scientists to replace undesirable genes with desirable ones. Debate continues over these techniques, and there is some mistrust of genetically modified (GM) organisms. Gene replacement therapies could prevent or cure genetic disorders, and research continues into possibilities and treatments.

1957 Soviet scientists launch the first artificial satellites to orbit Earth, *Sputnik I* and *Sputnik II*.

1958 U.S. electronic engineers invent integrated circuits, which enable a great reduction in the size of circuits for computers and other electronic devices.

1958 U.S. microbiologist John Enders produces a vaccine against measles.

1957

1958

1957 The rotary Wankel engine, invented by Felix Wankel, goes into production in West Germany.

1958 Scottish surgeon Ian Donald introduces the use of an ultrasound scan to examine an unborn baby in its mother's womb.

1958 In the United States, the National Aeronautics and Space Administration (NASA) is founded.

Lasers

A laser beam cuts metal more precisely than a saw. Lasers are used in delicate eye surgery, to measure distances, and without lasers there would have been no CDs or DVDs.

Among the most familiar uses of lasers are spectacular light shows.

TIMELINE
1959–1961

KEY:

- Biology and Medicine
- Engineering and Invention
- Astronomy and Math
- Chemistry and Physics

1959 Soviet scientists send three Lunik probes to the moon.

1959 The German company Voigtlander produces a zoom lens for its cameras.

1959

1959 British engineer Alec Issigonis designs the Mini car.

1959 French physician Jérôme Lejeune establishes that the condition Down syndrome is caused by a chromosome defect.

In 1917, Albert Einstein recognized it should be possible to stimulate atoms and molecules so they send out light. That is the principle behind the laser. It was not until the 1950s that physicists suggested a device that could generate a laser beam. In 1952, Charles H. Townes described a way to stimulate molecules of ammonia to give off microwave radiation using the principle of the maser (microwave amplification by stimulated emission of radiation). Townes built the first maser in 1953.

Timeline

1917 Einstein proposes stimulated emission

1952 Maser conceived

1958 Laser proposed in theory

1960 Maiman's ruby laser invented

The First Lasers

Microwave radiation is invisible, but in 1958, Townes and Arthur Schawlow showed it was theoretically possible to make a device to emit visible light. It would produce light amplification by stimulated emission of radiation—the laser. Theodore H. Maiman made the first laser in 1960.

Theodore Maiman made the world's first laser, emitted by a ruby crystal.

When a substance absorbs energy, its atoms or molecules jump from a low-energy level to a high-energy level. As they drop back to the low-energy level, they release surplus energy in the form of light. Ordinarily, each atom or molecule emits light independently of the others and at different wavelengths. But if the substance is exposed to very intense light of a particular wavelength

1960 Kenyan anthropologist Jonathan Leakey discovers remains of the oldest-known human, *Homo habilis* ("handy man"), in Tanzania.

1960 U.S. chemist Robert Woodward synthesizes the green plant pigment, chlorophyll.

1961 Soviet cosmonaut Yuri Gagarin becomes the first person in space.

1960

1961

1960 U.S. zoologists discover that bottle-nosed dolphins use a form of echolocation to detect objects underwater.

1960 U.S. physicist Theodore H. Maiman invents the ruby laser, the first practical laser.

1961 The U.S. company Texas Instruments produces the first silicon chips (for computers).

during its brief instant at the high-energy level, it will emit light at the same wavelength as the light shining on it. That is how the substance is stimulated, and stimulation further intensifies the light. The next step is to amplify the light by the use of mirrors. A mirror at one end of the device reflects light back through the substance being stimulated. A half-silvered mirror at the opposite end reflects some of the light but allows the remainder to escape as a laser beam.

A Focused Beam

A laser emits a narrow beam of light of a single wavelength—and therefore color—in which all the waves are in step. The light beam from a flashlight or car headlight diverges, so it illuminates a large area. A laser beam, however, is more focused. When it strikes a surface, the surface absorbs some of its energy and its temperature rises. Lasers produce such strong heat over such a small area that they can be used to trim excess material from electronic components and even to perform surgery on the retina at the back of the human eye.

Narrow laser beams can also measure distances. When a pulse strikes a surface, some of it is reflected. The speed of light is always the same, so distance is

One use of lasers is in barcode scanners. Barcodes changed the way people shop and how retail businesses are run.

TIMELINE
1961–1963

KEY:
- Biology and Medicine
- Engineering and Invention
- Astronomy and Math
- Chemistry and Physics

1961 U.S. chemists isolate the new radioactive element lawrencium.

1961 The IBM corporation markets the "golfball" typewriter.

1962 In her book *Silent Spring*, U.S. writer Rachel Carson highlights the damaging environmental effects of chemical pesticides.

1962 Astronaut John Glenn becomes the first American in space.

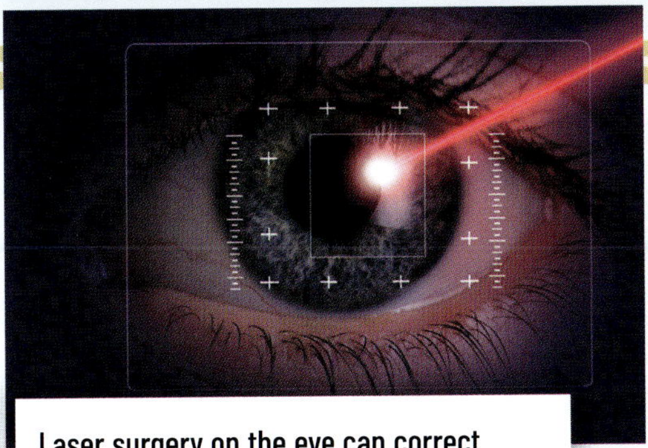

Laser surgery on the eye can correct optical defects in a matter of seconds.

calculated from the time that elapses between the emission of the pulse and the arrival of its reflection. This is called lidar (light radar). Lidar is used to measure the speed of moving objects, such as road traffic.

Producing the Ruby Laser

Both ends of a cylindrical rod of ruby crystal are polished flat and coated with silver to make a mirror at one end and a partial mirror at the other. The ruby is enclosed in a jacket to keep it cool. A spiral tube surrounding the ruby emits flashes of light. (Alternatively, the light can lie beside the ruby or be reflected onto it by mirrors.) Atoms in the ruby absorb energy from the tube and emit light. The laser beam emerges from the partially silvered end of the tube.

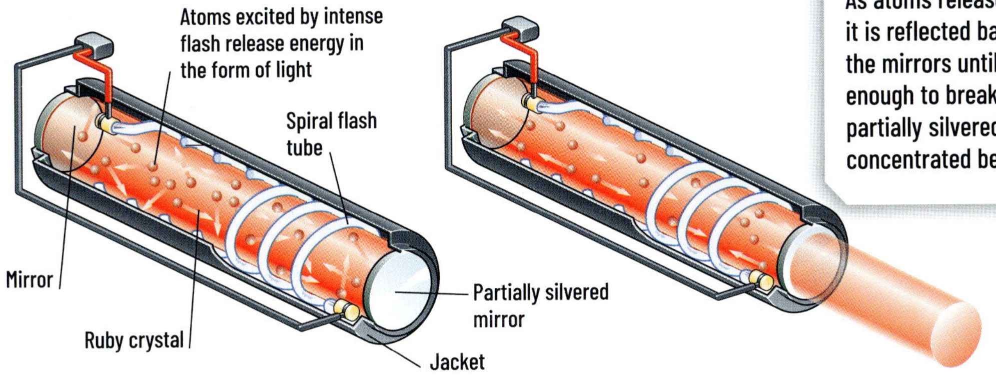

As atoms release more energy, it is reflected back and forth by the mirrors until it is powerful enough to break through the partially silvered mirror as a concentrated beam.

1962 The first pop-top can goes on sale in the United States.

1962 The 7-bit, 128-character American Standard Code for Information Interchange (ASCII) is introduced; it later becomes the international standard.

1963 Dutch company Philips introduces audiocassette tapes.

1963 British chemist Leslie Phillips develops a method of manufacturing carbon fibers.

1963 U.S. researchers develop the chemistry for producing "instant" color photographs.

Semiconductors

Modern cars are fitted with "chips" that perform lots of different tasks. Chips are all around us, but without semiconductors, they could not exist.

An integrated circuit has semiconductor devices—transistors, diodes, capacitors, and resistors—made as a single unit on a silicon chip.

TIMELINE
1964–1965

KEY:

- Engineering and Invention
- Astronomy and Math
- Chemistry and Physics

1964 NASA's probe *Mariner 4* sends back photographs of the surface of Mars.

1964 In Japan, the first bullet trains achieve speeds of 100 mph (160 km/h).

1964

1964 U.S. engineer Robert Moog invents a music synthesizer.

1964 The longest suspension bridge in the world at the time opens over the Verrazano Narrows between Brooklyn and Staten Island, New York.

Most metals conduct electricity well. Electrical wires are often made of copper, for example. Substances such as glass, paper, and rubber conduct electricity very badly and are used to insulate electrical wiring. Between these two groups is a class of substances called semiconductors. Germanium, tin, selenium, zinc, and tellurium are semiconducting elements, but silicon is by far the most widely used semiconductor material.

The First Semiconductor

When Guglielmo Marconi was experimenting with ways of converting an electrical current into radio waves, he needed a device to detect incoming radio signals. This rectifier, which allows a current to flow in one direction but not the other, was built by Ferdinand Braun in 1874. It was the first semiconductor device.

Rectifiers have two terminals, but advances in radio technology required devices with three terminals, allowing the current or voltage between two of the terminals to be controlled by the current or voltage applied to the third. The first three-terminal devices were vacuum tube triodes, called valves. Later versions had several triodes enclosed in the same tube. Valves used large amounts of power, became very hot, and their metal parts burned out, causing the valve to fail.

Timeline

1874 Braun's rectifier

1947 Point-contact transistor

1948 Audio amplifier

1948 Junction transistor

1958 Integrated circuit

1959 Planar technology

Old-style valves had to warm up before they would begin to work.

1964 U.S. radio astronomers Arno Penzias and Robert Wilson detect cosmic background microwave radiation, convincing most astronomers that the big bang theory is correct.

1965 The Mont Blanc road tunnel opens between France and Italy.

1964

1965

1965 American physicists Moo-Young Han and Yoichiro Nambu introduce "color" as a way of classifying some aspects of subatomic particles.

1965 Soviet cosmonaut Aleksi Leonov is the first person to walk in space.

Semiconductors

In a junction diode, current can flow only one way across the junction. There is a steady flow of holes and electrons to the junction; they neutralize each other. The positive and negative charges cancel and there is no charge overall. As a result, current flows freely. If the connections are reversed, the battery draws the electrons and holes away from the junction, and they can go no farther.

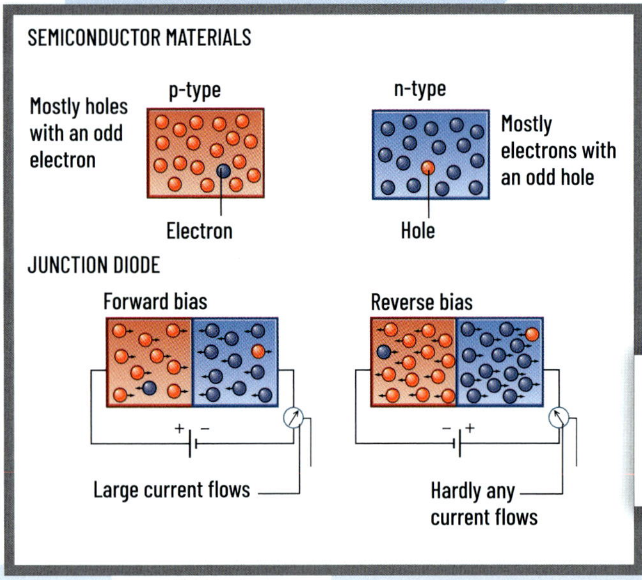

In 1947, physicists William Shockley, John Bardeen, and Walter Brattain made the first solid three-terminal device, a transistor, using germanium. They made several transistors in 1948, wiring them to other components to make an audio amplifier. Unlike valve amplifiers, this did not need to warm up to work. In 1948, Shockley made the junction transistor from slices of a semiconductor pressed together.

The presence of impurities in the germanium crystal improved its semiconductor properties. Modern semiconductors are made from slices of silicon crystal with tiny impurities.

The next development came in 1958. Jack Kilby, an electronic engineer working at Texas Instruments, realized that rather than making transistors one at a time, several

N-type semiconductors have free electrons; p-type semiconductors have vacancies (holes).

TIMELINE

1965–1967

KEY:

Biology and Medicine

Engineering and Invention

Astronomy and Math

1965 American Digital Equipment Corporation introduces the first minicomputer.

1966 Soviet and U.S. space probes land on the moon.

1966 Chinese and British engineers invent fiber-optic cable.

1965

1966

1966 U.S. inventor Stephanie Kwolek invents the ultrastrong synthetic fiber Kevlar. Five times stronger than steel, its uses include bulletproof vests.

Integrated circuits contain all the pieces of a traditional circuit board.

could be made together and placed on the same semiconductor. by overlaying different impurities. Other components could be added. Kilby had invented the integrated circuit.

Silicon Chips

A year later, at Fairchild Semiconductor Corporation, Jean Hoerni and Robert Noyce developed planar technology. This process spreads different layers onto a wafer of silicon to make a flat transistor, then places metal strips onto the surface to make the necessary connections.

The chips in computers and other modern electronic devices are smaller than postage stamps. Plastic cases enclose layers of transistors and related components, and the wiring linking them, on the surface of a sliver of silicon. They are integrated circuits based on semiconductor technology.

Adding Impurities

"Doping" an element with impurities produces n- or p-type semiconductors. The first have free electrons; the second have vacancies (holes) carrying a positive charge. When a current is applied, electrons and holes move in opposite directions through the semiconductor.

The junction transistor has three layers of materials, p-n-p or n-p-n. A small current applied to the middle piece (the base) controls a larger current between the outer pieces (the emitter and the collector).

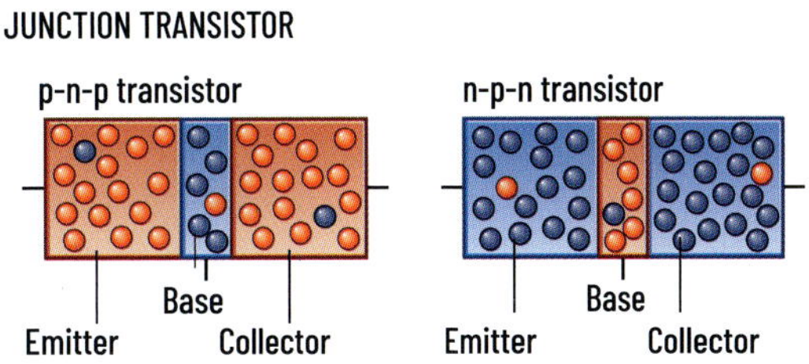

A junction transistor can be used in amplifiers and other circuits.

1966 An electronic fuel injection system for automobile engines is invented in Britain.

1967 Three U.S. astronauts die in a fire during a ground test of an Apollo spacecraft.

1967 South African surgeon Christiaan Barnard performs the first human heart transplant operation. The patient lives for 18 days with the new heart.

1966

1967

1967 British astronomers Jocelyn Bell Burnell and Antony Hewish detect the first pulsar.

1967 The U.S. company Raytheon markets the first domestic microwave oven.

The Apollo Program

In 1961, President John F. Kennedy pledged the United States would land a person on the moon within 10 years. In July 1969, two astronauts fulfilled that promise.

The astronauts from *Apollo 11* erect a flag on the moon. The flag is supported by wire as there is no wind to blow it open.

TIMELINE
1968–1969

KEY:
- Biology and Medicine
- Engineering and Invention
- Astronomy and Math
- Chemistry and Physics

1968 NASA's *Apollo 7* orbits Earth; *Apollo 8* orbits the moon.

1968 Italian-American inventor Candido Jacuzzi invents the whirlpool bath named for him.

1968

1968 The Lockheed C-5 Galaxy becomes the largest airplane in the world.

1968 U.S. computer engineer Douglas Engelbart devises the computer mouse.

The spacecraft that launched the *Apollo 11* astronauts to the moon had four main parts. The Saturn V rocket propelled the whole machine into space; the command module, Columbia, housed the three astronauts; the service module contained the main propulsion rockets for the journey; and below that was the lunar module, Eagle. The lunar module carried two of the three astronauts down to land on the moon's surface on the Sea of Tranquility. After they had completed their surface mission, the astronauts took off again in Eagle, which returned to dock with the orbiting command module. Just eight days later, it parachuted into the Pacific Ocean.

Timeline

1967 January: Three Apollo astronauts die in ground fire

1968 October: *Apollo 7* in Earth orbit

1968 December: *Apollo 8* orbits the moon

1969 March: *Apollo 9* tests lunar module in Earth orbit

1969 May: *Apollo 10* tests lunar module in moon orbit

1969 July: *Apollo 11* lands on the moon

The Apollo Program

The earlier Apollo missions had tested various launch procedures, rockets, and modules—at first in Earth orbit, then around the moon—before making the final landing. In January 1967, the first planned Apollo flight ended in disaster when three astronauts died in a fire during a launch pad test. The next year, NASA (National Aeronautics and Space Administration) made three uncrewed launches.

Apollo 11 lifts off in 1969. The top of the giant Saturn V rocket carried the command, service, and lunar modules and an escape tower, which could blast away the command module and crew in case of an emergency.

1969 *Apollo 11* makes the first crewed moon landing.

1969 English chemist Dorothy Hodgkin uses X-ray crystallography to work out the molecular structure of insulin.

1969

1969 The Anglo-French supersonic airliner Concorde makes its maiden flight in France.

1969 English scientists Robert Edwards and Patrick Steptoe fertilize the first human eggs in vitro.

Stepping Stones to the Moon and Back

Apollo 11 took off on July 16, 1969. The three stages of the Saturn V rocket fired (1, 2, 3) to send the spacecraft into Earth orbit and launch the modules on the trajectory to the moon (4). Once in moon orbit, the lunar module separated from the command module (5) and descended to the surface (6). After the landing, the top part of the lunar module took off (7) and rejoined the command module (8), which then followed the transearth trajectory. After jettisoning the lunar module (9), the command module reentered Earth atmosphere (10) and parachuted into the Pacific Ocean (11).

In October 1968, *Apollo 7* carried three astronauts on a 163-orbit flight around Earth. Two months later, *Apollo 8* took three astronauts to the moon, making ten orbits. In March 1969, the lunar module was tested in Earth orbit by *Apollo 9*, and in May, two *Apollo 10* astronauts tested it in orbit around the moon.

The Moon Landing

Apollo 11 lifted off in July 1969 crewed by Neil Armstrong, Edwin (Buzz) Aldrin, and Michael Collins. It reached the moon without a hitch. Armstrong and Aldrin descended to the surface in the lunar module on July 20, spending two hours taking photographs and collecting samples. They erected a U.S. flag and left a plaque marking their mission.

This diagram shows the stages of the Saturn V rocket and the moon mission.

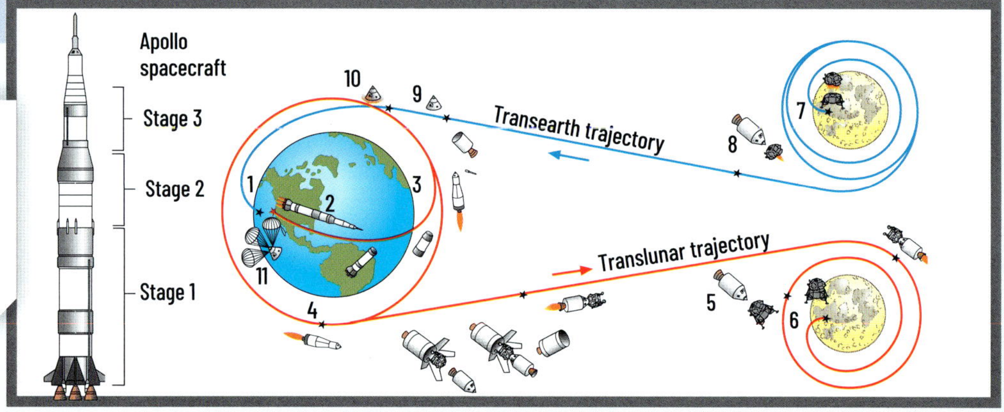

TIMELINE
1970–1972

KEY:
Biology and Medicine
Engineering and Invention
Astronomy and Math

1970

1970 Floppy disk data storage media comes into use for computers.

1970 Fossil finds in Antarctica, Africa, and India provide evidence for the theory of continental drift (because these landmasses must once have been joined).

1970 The 400-seat Boeing 747 jumbo jet goes into service.

1970 NASA's *Apollo 13* mission is abandoned after an accident in space, but the crew return safely to Earth.

Earth rises above the surface of the moon in a photo taken from *Apollo 11*.

The Apollo Modules

During take-off and reentry, the crew stayed in the command module. The attached service module contained the engine and fuel to propel the mission to the moon and back. The lunar module had two sections: The lower section stayed on the moon while the upper part carried the crew back to the orbiting command module. The lunar module and service modules were jettisoned, allowing the command module to reenter Earth's atmosphere and splash down.

Later Missions

Apollo 12 also landed on the moon in November 1969, but the mission of *Apollo 13* in April 1970 was a near-disaster. An explosion in the service module cut off power and oxygen, but the crew still made a safe return.

In December 1972, *Apollo 17* was NASA's last crewed trip to the moon. The Apollo program had cost in total about $25 billion.

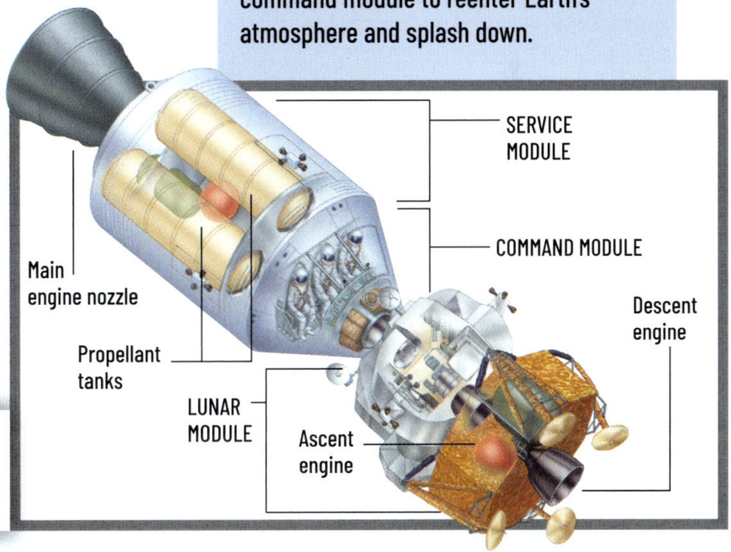

The service, command, and lunar modules configured for moon orbit.

1971 Chinese American biochemist Choh Hao Li synthesizes the human growth hormone.

1971 U.S. electronic engineer Ted Hoff and colleagues introduce a single-chip microprocessor (the Intel 4004).

1972 The computer company Atari, Inc., creates the popular video game Pong. It is followed a year later by the first computer game for the general public.

1971

1972

1971 NASA space probe *Mariner 9* goes into orbit around Mars.

1971 U.S. companies Texas Instruments and Intel Corporation produce pocket calculators.

1972 Kenyan anthropologist Richard Leakey finds an intact skull of a 1.9-million-year-old human ancestor, *Homo habilis*.

The Space Shuttle

The story of the space shuttle is one of triumph and tragedy. It was involved in some of NASA's greatest space achievements as well as in its two worst disasters.

The space shuttle *Challenger* leaves Dryden Flight Research Center, California, atop NASA's Boeing 747 carrier aircraft on its way to the Kennedy Space Center, Florida, for its first launch. *Challenger* made its first space flight in 1981.

TIMELINE

1972–1974

KEY:

- Biology and Medicine
- Engineering and Invention
- Astronomy and Math
- Chemistry and Physics

1972 French mathematician René Thom introduces catastrophe theory, which soon has applications in physics.

1972 U.S. theoretical physicist Murray Gell-Mann develops a new branch of physics, quantum chromodynamics (QCD). It describes nuclear interaction in terms of quarks.

1973 Physicists at Bell Laboratories produce a continuous-wave laser that can be tuned to different wavelengths.

1973 U.S. and English physicists begin to develop nuclear magnetic resonance imaging (MRI scanning), later used in medical analysis.

Plans for the space shuttle date back to 1972. NASA wanted a cargo-carrying spacecraft that could launch into space, carry out its mission, and then return to base to land on its own and be used again and again. It was hoped the shuttle would fly up to 50 missions a year, but in reality it flew only about eight.

At launch, the shuttle consisted of three parts. The airplanelike orbiter was 122 feet (37 m) long and had three main engines fueled by liquid oxygen and liquid hydrogen. The large external tank held extra fuel, and two 148-foot (45 m) solid rocket boosters attached to either side of it. The flight deck had seats for up to seven crew, and the middeck served as a wardroom, kitchen, and gym, and also had a toilet. The 59-foot (18 m) payload bay carried up to 27.6 tons (25 t). The bay also had a robot arm to deploy and retrieve payloads. It also acted as a "ladder" for spacewalking astronauts.

Endeavour docked at the International Space Station.

Timeline

1983 *Challenger*: Sally Ride becomes first American woman in space

1990 *Discovery:* Places the Hubble Space Telescope in Earth orbit

1995 *Atlantis:* 100th U.S. crewed flight

1996 *Atlantis:* Docks with Soviet space station Mir

1996 *Columbia:* At almost 17 days, longest space shuttle mission

1998 *Endeavour:* Takes up second module of new International Space Station

2002 *Columbia:* Upgrades the Hubble Space Telescope

2005 *Discovery:* Docks with the new International Space Station

1973 The first teletext systems are broadcast on British television.

1973 NASA space probe *Pioneer 10* flies past Jupiter.

1974 U.S. company General Motors introduces catalytic convertors for cars.

1974 NASA space probe *Mariner 10* reaches Mercury.

1974 U.S. chemical engineer Arthur Fry invents the semiadhesive Post-it Note.

1974 U.S. scientists issue warnings about the damage CFCs (chlorofluorocarbons) are doing to Earth's ozone layer.

1973 — 1974

Shuttle Missions

NASA built six space shuttles. The first, *Enterprise* of 1977, was never launched into space. In 1981, *Columbia* became the first shuttle to make an orbital flight, followed by *Challenger* in 1983, *Discovery* in 1984, and *Atlantis* in 1985. In 1986, *Challenger* exploded soon after launch, killing all seven crew members. NASA then built *Endeavour*, which first flew

After liftoff (1), the shuttle accelerated upward (2) for two minutes before dropping the spent booster rockets (3), which parachuted down to be recovered. About eight minutes into the flight (4), the shuttle entered Earth orbit and jettisoned the external fuel tank (5), which burned up on reentry. After its space mission (6), the shuttle turned around (7), fired its rockets for braking (8), and reentered Earth's atmosphere (9). After turning again (10), it swung from side to side (11, 12) to lose speed before making the landing approach (13) and gliding down (14) to land on its wheels (15), stopping with the aid of a braking parachute. The carrier aircraft (16) took the shuttle back to Edwards Air Force Base to prepare it for the next space shuttle flight.

TIMELINE

1975–1977

KEY:

Biology and Medicine

Engineering and Invention

Astronomy and Math

1975 British pharmacologists discover enkephalins, chemicals produced in the brain that control pain.

1975 U.S. engineer Edward Roberts markets the first commercial personal computer (PC), the Altair 8800.

1975

1975 Soviet and U.S. space capsules link up in Earth orbit.

1975 U.S. computer programmers Bill Gates and Paul Allen found the Microsoft Corporation.

The Hubble Space Telescope undergoes repairs in the shuttle's cargo bay.

in 1992. In 2003, the shuttle had its second disaster when *Columbia* disintegrated 16 minutes before it was due to land. All the crew died. After a major refit, *Discovery* restarted the shuttle program in July 2005. It docked with the International Space Station (launched in 1998), and the crew inspected damage to the craft's tiles caused by a piece of insulating foam that broke off the external tank during liftoff. NASA grounded the fleet while investigating the tile problem.

The shuttle program resumed in August 2009, with a *Discovery* mission. The final shuttle launch was by the *Atlantis* module and took place in 2011.

The *Challenger* Disaster

The explosion of *Challenger* some 73 seconds after liftoff in 1986 was an enduring moment in space exploration. Many Americans were watching the launch live. They included students following Christa McAuliffe, a teacher recruited by NASA to interest children in the mission. The cause of the disaster was traced to a failed seal in one of the solid rocket boosters, probably itself caused by the extremely cold temperatures at the launch site.

Workers recover part of the *Challenger* after the shuttle disaster of 1986.

1976 The supersonic airliner Concorde begins commercial service flights.

1976 U.S. physiologist Roger Guillemin reports the existence of endorphins, morphinelike chemicals released in the brain to control pain.

1977 U.S. astronomers observe the rings of Uranus.

1976 In Japan, the Matsushita company introduces the VHS format for videocassettes.

1976 U.S. computer designers Steven Jobs and Stephen Wozniak found the computer company Apple.

1977 A pedal-powered airplane, *Gossamer Condor*, makes a controlled flight of over 1 mile (1.6 km).

Personal Computers

In just 20 years, the personal computer progressed from being a novelty item for enthusiasts to an essential tool that is used every day in households all over the world.

Today, laptop and desktop computers are familiar in virtually every home.

TIMELINE
1977–1979

KEY:

- Biology and Medicine
- Engineering and Invention
- Astronomy and Math
- Chemistry and Physics

1977 U.S. government scientists develop a neutron bomb.

1977 A team led by British biochemists explains the first full sequence of DNA bases (of a virus).

1978 Astronomers in the United States locate Pluto's moon Charon.

1978 The U.S. government bans the use of chlorofluorocarbons in aerosol cans.

A personal computer (PC) is one of the most versatile and useful devices in homes all over the world. Yet PCs are fairly new. The first fully electronic computer was built in 1946 at the University of Pennsylvania. All the early computers used vacuum tubes, or valves. Those machines were so huge that they filled a large room, and they were unreliable (because of tube failures). The invention of the transistor in 1947 offered a smaller, more dependable replacement for the vacuum tube, and the invention of the integrated circuit in 1958 opened up the possibility of miniaturization. Computers began to shrink in size.

Computer for the Home

It was not until 1975 that a computer appeared that was both affordable and small enough to use at home. Micro Instrumentation and Telemetry Systems (MITS) of Albuquerque, New Mexico, sold the Altair 8800 for $495 assembled, and in kit form for just $395. The computer came without a monitor, keyboard, or printer—and it had only 256 bytes of memory.

The invention of the integrated circuit, following on from the invention of the transistor, was critical to the development of modern personal computers.

Timeline

1946 ENIAC

1947 Transistor

1958 Integrated circuit

1964 BASIC programming language

1972 CP/M operating system for small computers

1975 Altair 8800

1980 MS-DOS

1980 ZX80

1981 IBM's first PC

1990 World Wide Web

1978

1978 The first "test tube" baby is born in England.

1978 U.S. surgeon Robert Jarvik devises the Jarvik-7 artificial heart.

1979

1979 Digital compact disks (CDs) are developed independently in Japan and the Netherlands.

1979 The Swedish company Ericsson markets the first cellular telephones (mobile phones).

1979 The earliest cases of the disease that becomes known as AIDS (acquired immunodeficiency syndrome) occur in the United States.

1979 The World Health Organization announces that smallpox has been eradicated worldwide.

Hard Disk Drive

Backup memory that needs to be rapidly accessed can be stored on hard disks inside a computer's disk drive. Data is stored as magnetic fields in areas as small as 40-millionths of an inch (1 micrometer) across. Read/write heads mounted on the ends of arms swing in and out across each disk as required, "flying" a few millionths of an inch above the disk surface on a cushion of air. A carriage moves the head in and out.

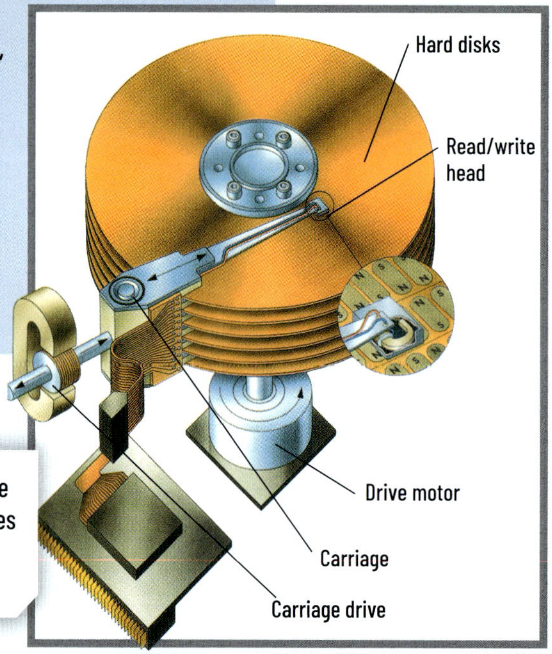

Hard disks can rotate at speeds of 100 miles per hour (160 km/h) or more.

Computer Software

Computer software—the programs that run useful applications such as word processing or games—will work only if the computer is able to communicate with a storage device such as a disk drive. This process requires special software in the form of an operating system. In 1972, American computer scientist Gary Kildall (1942–1994) came up with PL/M (Programming Language/ Microprocessor). The following year, Kildall wrote software that allowed the user to read data files stored on a disk and write files onto the disk. It was the first operating system for small computers. DOS was a rival system developed by Bill Gates of Microsoft in 1980.

Computers remained expensive, however, until 1980, when Clive

TIMELINE

1980–1981

KEY:

Biology and Medicine

Engineering and Invention

Astronomy and Math

1980 The U.S. Supreme Court rules that genetically engineered life forms can be patented.

1980 U.S. father and son Luis and Walter Alvarez suggest that a meteorite collision with Earth may have led to the extinction of the dinosaurs.

1980

1980 Sony in Japan and Philips in the Netherlands market the audio compact disk (CD) for commercial use.

1980 Polish-American mathematician Benoit Mandlebrot investigates fractals, which are mathematical curves generated by successive subdivision.

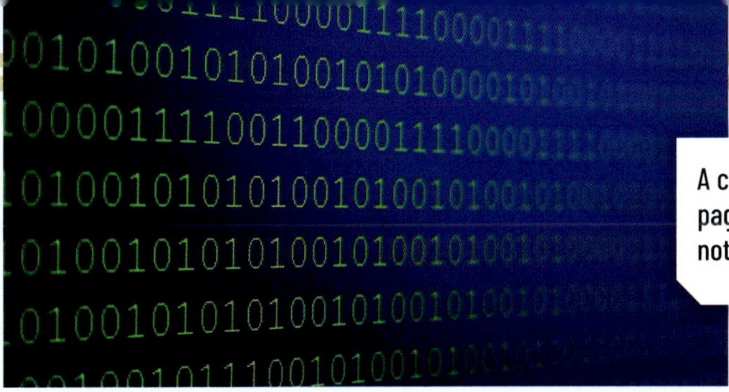

A computer program is page after page of binary notation: 0s and 1s.

Sinclair designed the ZX80. In the United States, it cost $199.95 ready-made and connected to a TV receiver. IBM introduced its first small computer in 1981, calling it a "personal computer" (PC). Within a year or two, rival manufacturers were marketing cheaper imitations, known as "IBM clones." All of them were similar to the IBM PC and used MS-DOS. Modern PCs are the direct descendents of the "clones."

Better Processors

The power of a PC depends on the speed of its processor and the amount of memory it has. Both have increased rapidly and continue to do so, allowing modern computers to perform tasks far beyond the capacity of their predecessors. The first multimedia PC appeared in 1991, and English computer scientist Tim Berners-Lee created the World Wide Web in 1990. Today, computers of various kinds are key to our daily lives, such as in the operation of household items and many forms of transport, as well as being used for education and entertainment.

This early hard drive comprised a stack of hard disks mounted on the same spindle, which could all be accessed simultaneously.

1981 U.S. authorities first acknowledge acquired immune deficiency syndrome (AIDS) as a communicable disease.

1981 NASA's first space shuttle, *Columbia*, makes its maiden flight, proving that a reusable spacecraft is practicable.

1981

1981 U.S. company Hewlett Packard launches a 32-bit silicon chip for its computers.

1981 French railroad company SNCF introduces its new high-speed train, the TGV (Train à Grande Vitesse).

Cloning Animals

In 1996, a lamb named Dolly was born by genetic engineering. But she was not the first cloned animal. The science of cloning has a surprisingly long history.

Ian Wilmut pictured with his creation, Dolly, the world's first cloned sheep.

TIMELINE
1982–1984

KEY:

Biology and Medicine

Engineering and Invention

Astronomy and Math

1982 Two Soviet space probes reach Venus and sample the atmosphere.

1982 Engineers in California complete the world's largest solar power plant, Solar One.

1982

1982 Biochemists produce the first totally synthetic vaccine (against diphtheria).

1982 Biologist Karl Setter discovers bacteria living in hot seawater near black smokers on the seabed.

In 1892, Hans Driesch watched a fertilized sea urchin egg divide into two cells under a microscope. He then shook the tiny embryo until the two cells came apart. Each one went on to develop into a normal urchin larva. He had created identical twins, or clones.

First Steps

In 1902, Hans Spemann took things a step further. He split a two-cell salamander embryo. Over the next four decades, Spemann continued to investigate the possibilities of cloning. He predicted that one day it would be possible to create clones by transferring a nucleus from an adult cell into an egg cell from which the original nucleus had been removed. This means that instead of being a genetic blend of two parents, the newly created embryo would be an exact replica of the adult animal from which the original cell came.

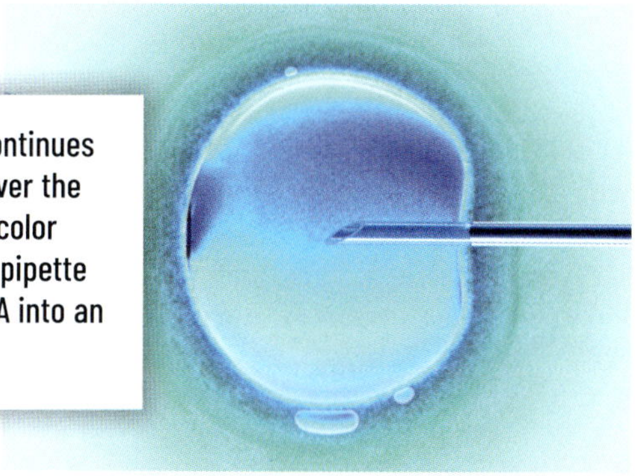

Genetic research continues in laboratories all over the world. In this false-color magnified image, a pipette is used to inject DNA into an unfertilized egg.

Timeline

1892 German embryologist Hans Driesch creates cloned sea urchin larva

1902 German embryologist Hans Spemann creates salamander clones

1952 Robert Briggs and Thomas J. King clone a frog using a nucleus from an embryo cell

1958 Scientists at Oxford University clone a frog using a nucleus from an adult cell

1963 The word "clone" is first used

1984 First mammal clone

1986 Dolly the sheep

1983 U.S. mathematicians announce a new way of finding prime numbers.

1983 French virologist Luc Montagnier and U.S. physician Robert Gallo discover the human immunodeficiency virus (HIV) that causes AIDS.

1984 U.S. biologist Robert Sinsheimer proposes the setting up of the Human Genome Project.

1983

1984

1983 U.S. company Apple markets a home computer that features a mouse and pull-down menus.

1983 U.S. astronaut Sally Ride becomes the first American woman in space.

1984 English geneticist Alec Jeffreys perfects the technique of genetic fingerprinting.

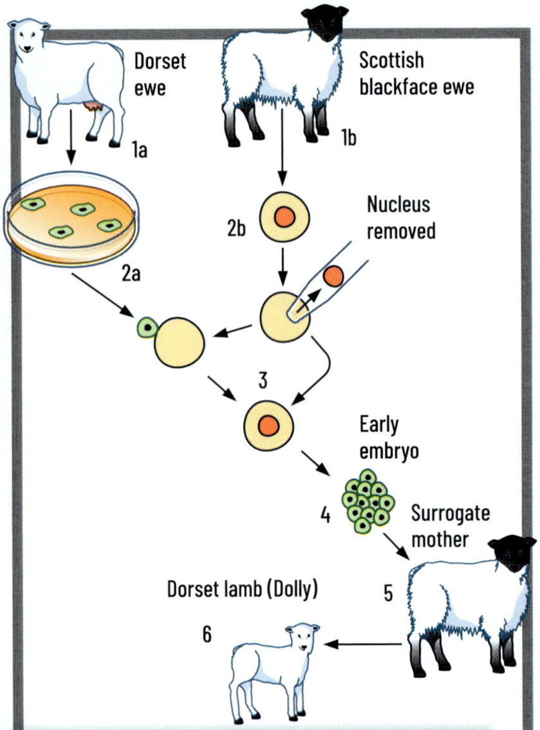

Cells are removed from a Dorset ewe (1a) and DNA replication starts (2a). An egg is removed from a Scottish blackface ewe (1b) and its nucleus is removed (2b). The nucleus from one of the Dorset ewe cells is fused with the egg (3). The cell divides to form an embryo (4), which is placed into a ewe (5). Dolly is identical to the nucleus donor (6).

Spemann's prediction became reality in two stages. In 1952, Robert Briggs and Thomas J. King removed a cell from a northern leopard frog embryo and transferred it into an unfertilized frog egg cell from which the nucleus had been removed. The clone developed normally.

Then, in 1958, scientists at Oxford University, England, succeeded in performing a similar procedure, but this time using a nucleus from an adult cell. The fact that the donor cells were fully mature and thus separate from one another was important, because it proved that adult cells keep a full set of genetic material despite the fact that only part of this material is expressed.

The term "clone" was coined by John Burdon Haldane in 1963. It comes from the Greek word for "twig."

Breakthrough?

In 1977, a scientist at the University of Geneva caused a sensation when he claimed to have cloned three mice. Karl Illmensee said he had used much the same nuclear transfer techniques as those previously

TIMELINE
1984–1986

KEY:

Biology and Medicine

Engineering and Invention

Astronomy and Math

Chemistry and Physics

1984 Apple sells the first Macintosh computers.

1984 Microsoft launches the Windows computer applications program for PCs.

1985 British scientists detect a hole in the ozone layer above Antarctica. It is blamed on chlorofluorocarbons (CFCs) in the atmosphere.

1985 Several chemists collaborate to produce a new allotrope of carbon, buckminsterfullerene or "buckyballs."

employed to create the amphibian clones. Other scientists were incredulous because mammalian cells are much smaller, and nobody could understand how he had managed to manipulate them. Illmensee was not able to satisfy his many critics and his claim came to be regarded as a fraud.

Cloning Mammals

The first reliably documented mammal clone was produced in 1984 by a research group at Cambridge University led by Steen Willadsen. Willadsen and his colleagues cloned a sheep by transferring the nucleus of an embryonic sheep cell into an empty egg. Two years later, Ian Wilmut began work in Edinburgh, Scotland. Wilmut was to become famous as the man who created "Dolly the sheep." Dolly went on to bear six lambs of her own in the normal way, but her health was poor. Since Dolly, many more mammals have been cloned. In 1997, Wilmut created Polly, a sheep cloned from fetal cells genetically altered to include a human gene. Other cloned animals include pigs, cattle, mice, and a racehorse.

Human Clones

Human clones already exist. Identical twins are natural clones formed when an early embryo splits in half. But the possibility of artificially cloning humans has stirred up a heated ethical debate. On the one hand, medical benefits could be huge. They could have applications in the treatment of conditions such as Parkinson's disease and diabetes. On the other hand, the prospect of creating life to order or creating clones to replace loved ones is disturbing to many people.

This litter of cloned pigs was created in 2001 to help with medical research.

1985 Japanese company Minolta launches the world's first autofocus single-lens reflex (SLR) camera.

1985 Sony and Philips invent the CD-ROM (compact disc read-only memory) to store digital media.

1986 Space shuttle *Challenger* blows up soon after takeoff, killing all seven crew members.

1986 Japanese manufacturers demonstrate a digital audio tape (DAT) system.

1986 In the United States, the first field trials are carried out with genetically engineered crops (tobacco).

1986 European space probe *Giotto* passes within 375 miles (600 km) of Halley's comet.

1985

1986

Global Warming

The greenhouse effect is a natural phenomenon that makes our planet habitable. However, human activities are upsetting the balance and speeding up global warming.

Factory gases and car exhausts are leading contributors to global warming.

TIMELINE
1987–1988

KEY:
- Biology and Medicine
- Engineering and Invention
- Astronomy and Math
- Chemistry and Physics

1987 Japanese airlines introduce air-to-ground satellite telephones.

1987 German chemists make an electrically conducting plastic by "doping" polythene with iodine.

1987

1987 Soviet cosmonaut Yuri Romanenko spends a record 326 days on the space station Mir.

1987 British surgeons carry out the first heart/lung/liver triple transplant operation.

One consequence of rising temperatures is the melting of the polar ice caps.

The greenhouse effect is nothing new. Earth has benefited from it for billions of years. The overall effect is an insulating one—the natural greenhouse effect keeps Earth's average temperature at about 30 degrees higher than it would otherwise be.

Changes in Climate

During the early 20th century, scientists knew that Earth's climate had previously undergone dramatic changes and that it was currently enjoying a period of relative warmth, called an interglacial period. In the late-19th century, Swedish physical chemist Svante Arrhenius had identified the greenhouse role of carbon dioxide (CO_2), and had suspected that cooling events (ice ages) might have been caused by reduced levels of atmospheric CO_2. He calculated the amount of CO_2 released by human activities and realized that, over a prolonged period of time, such output could begin to

Timeline

1827 Fourier describes the greenhouse effect

1896 Arrhenius publishes a theory of global warming

1939 Callendar observes a rise in global temperatures and CO_2 levels

1979 The first World Climate Conference

1985 First international conference on the greenhouse effect (Villach, Austria)

1988 United Nations sets up the Intergovernmental Panel on Climate Change (IPCC)

2005 Kyoto Protocol comes into effect

2016 Paris Agreement signed

2023 Hottest year on record, to date

1988 The Human Genome Organization (HUGO) is set up to promote international collaboration in the field of human genetics.

1988 U.S. climatologist James Hansen predicts that "greenhouse gases" in the atmosphere will lead to global warming.

1988

1988 The U.S. Patent Office grants a patent for a genetically engineered mouse.

1988 ISDN (integrated services digital network) is launched in Japan as a world standard for digital communications.

Greenhouse Effect

Some solar radiation is bounced straight out into space by gases in the atmosphere. But a lot passes through and hits Earth's surface. Some is absorbed, and some is reflected. The reflected heat (albedo) takes the form of long-wave infrared radiation. Gas molecules in the atmosphere absorb the radiation and keep it from being lost into space. The gas particles begin to reradiate energy in all directions. About 30 percent is radiated back downward to Earth's surface.

Excess carbon dioxide absorbs solar energy, trapping the heat near Earth.

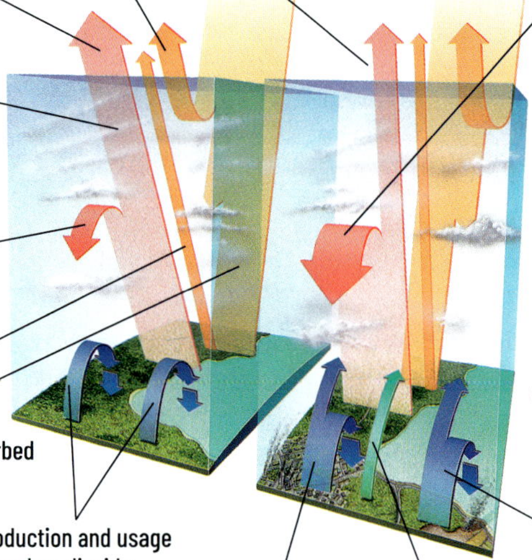

TIMELINE
1989–1990

KEY:

Biology and Medicine

Engineering and Invention

Astronomy and Math

1989 The *Voyager* 2 space probe reveals that Neptune has a system of rings.

1990 NASA places the Hubble Space Telescope in orbit around Earth. It will provide astronomers with detailed images of astronomical objects.

1989

1990

1989 The oil tanker *Exxon Valdez* runs aground off Alaska, causing an environmental disaster.

1989 U.S. computer engineer Seymour Cray sets up a company to build the Cray 3 supercomputer.

have the reverse effect. In 1896, he was the first to suggest that, instead of facing global cooling, the world might experience global warming as a result of industrial emissions. This idea was revived in 1939 by Guy Stewart Callendar. He suggested that increases in temperatures and CO_2 levels were linked. From then onward, the idea refused to go away.

Most scientists now accept that global warming is causing droughts and floods. But some people continue to argue that it is simply part of a natural cycle.

Global Warming

In the 1960s, it became possible to measure accurately atmospheric carbon dioxide levels. It became clear they were rising rapidly. Climate models began to take account of variables such as ocean absorption and clouds. The year 1988 marked a turning point. Globally, it was the hottest year on record at the time (and there have been many hotter ones since), and was the year that public awareness of global warming took off. Between 1890 and 1990, the amount of CO_2 in the atmosphere rose by a quarter from 280 to 345 parts per million by volume. By the end of the 20th century, most scientists accepted that the significant warming was a result of human activities. In 1997, 84 nations agreed to curb emissions by signing the Kyoto Protocol. This was superseded in November 2016 by the Paris Agreement, negotiated by 196 parties and covering climate change mitigation, adaptation, and finance. Regular international conferences are held to discuss the issues, but the aim of keeping global warming to a target limit of 2.7°F (1.5°C) looks to be a difficult challenge.

1990 English computer scientist Tim Berners-Lee begins to devise the World Wide Web.

1990 The Human Genome Project begins, directed by U.S. biophysicist James Watson.

1990

1990 British and French engineers meet beneath the English Channel as they complete drilling for the Channel Tunnel.

1990 U.S. company Kodak announces the invention of a Photo CD disk.

The World Wide Web

The dream of a universal information database was realized in 1990 with the launch of the World Wide Web. Users have access to a vast amount of data instantly.

Internet servers contain huge amounts of information in highly secure environments.

TIMELINE
1991–1992

KEY:

- Biology and Medicine
- Engineering and Invention
- Astronomy and Math
- Chemistry and Physics

1991 Japanese researcher Sumio Iijima makes carbon nanotubes.

1991 U.S. electronics engineer Kenneth Matsumura invents a small electrocardiograph machine that warns the wearer of heart problems.

1991

1991 European researchers briefly achieve controlled nuclear fusion.

1991 English inventor Trevor Baylis invents a clockwork radio for use in places with no electricity supply and few batteries.

The World Wide Web uses telephone lines or radio to link computers into a network that extends across the world. The Web allows computer users to gain immediate access to billions of pages of documents as well as video, movies, and music. Tim Berners-Lee devised the Web in 1990.

Early Connections

Computer links had existed since the 1970s. In 1981, the City University of New York launched BITNET (the "BIT" standing for "because it's time"). EUNET followed in 1982. These networks were limited by the difficulty of generating information on one computer in a form that could be read by other computers. The problem was solved within networks, but one network was unable to communicate with computers belonging to another.

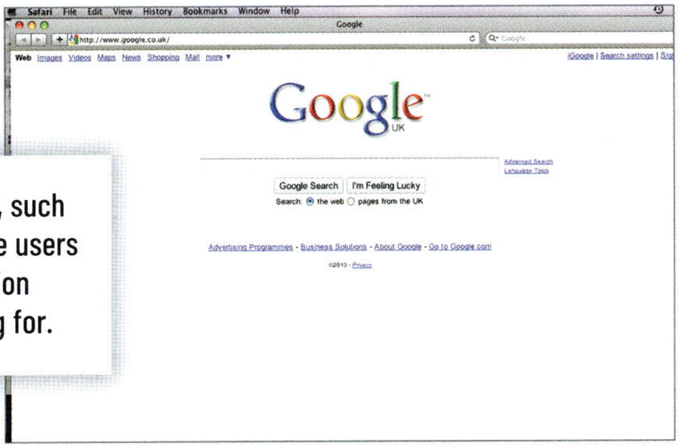

Search engines, such as Google, guide users to the information they are looking for.

Timeline

1980 Tim Berners-Lee releases Enquire

1981 BITNET launched

1982 EUNET launched; internet born

1984 EARN launched; domain names introduced; JANET launched

1985 NSFNET launched

1990 Tim Berners-Lee names the World Wide Web

1991 NSFNET opened to the public; the Web released to the public

1992 "Information superhighway project"

1993 Mosaic X, the first Web browser, introduced

1993 World Wide Web certified by CERN as being in the public domain

1992 Experimental digital radio broadcasts begin in France.

1992 NASA scientists detect "ripples" in cosmic background radiation (caused by minute temperature variations).

1992

1992 Dutch company Philips makes the interactive CD-I computer disk.

1992 U.S. research scientists make extra-hard diamonds using the isotope carbon-13 (natural diamonds are made from carbon-12).

Domain Name Servers

To receive messages, each host has a unique address. In 1984, this system introduced domain name servers. A domain name server stores lists of domain names and can route requests accordingly. Domain names include http:// (hypertext transfer protocol), www (World Wide Web), ac (academic), edu (education), com (commercial), and gov (government), as well as national identifiers, such as uk (United Kingdom), de (Germany), fr (France), and nl (Netherlands).

http:// is one of the most familiar of all the domain names in use on the internet.

As early as 1974, computer scientists had devised a system called a transmission control protocol/internet protocol (TCP/IP) to allow computers to send data between networks. Henceforth, networks could be linked: The internet had been born, and with it, e-mail. A computer linked to a network is called a host, and e-mail proved so popular that, by 1984, there were more than 1,000 hosts generating a high volume of traffic.

Communication Growth

The internet received a further boost in 1984 when the UK government backed JANET (Joint Academic Network) to serve British universities. In 1985, the U.S. National Science Foundation set up NSFNET to extend internet use to authorized persons on every U.S. campus. In 1988, NSFNET upgraded the network capacity from 56,000 to 1.544 million bytes per second. Following the opening of NSFNET, the number of internet users grew from about 5,000 in 1986 to 28,000 in 1987, although only people in research or education could access the network. In 1991, NSFNET allowed access to private computers. In 1992, U.S. Senator Al Gore

TIMELINE
1993–1995

KEY:
- Biology and Medicine
- Engineering and Invention
- Astronomy and Math
- Chemistry and Physics

1993 U.S. physicians introduce gene therapy for the congenital disorder cystic fibrosis.

1993 Japanese company Mazda announces plans to construct a fuel-efficient car using a Miller-cycle internal combustion engine.

1993

1993 U.S. company Intel markets the Pentium microprocessor chip for computers.

1993 U.S. astronomers Carolyn Shoemaker and David Levy discover a new comet, Shoemaker-Levy 9.

introduced the High-Performance Computing Act, nicknamed the "information superhighway project."

World Wide Web

Since 1980, English scientist Tim Berners-Lee had been a software developer at the European Organization for Nuclear Research (CERN) in Switzerland. He was looking for a way to allow communication between physicists in different countries using different computer systems. By 1991, he had written a program to achieve this; he named it the World Wide Web.

Berners-Lee released the program to CERN workers, and in August 1991, the program was published on the internet, free for anyone. The World Wide Web was born—but it grew slowly. By the end of 1993, there were only about 150 sites. Then, also in 1993, Mark Andreessen of the National Center for Supercomputing Applications released the first browser, Mosaic X (later renamed Netscape). Browsers give users a visual way to navigate and interact with documents. Where the internet linked computers, the World Wide Web linked documents. Today, there are more than 1.13 billion websites and over 30 billion indexed Web pages.

Broadband and wireless systems mean that rapid access to the internet can be achieved with portable devices from virtually anywhere in the world.

1994 For the first time, more computers than TV sets are sold throughout the world.

1994 U.S. scientists at Fermilab announce the discovery of the evasive subatomic particle called the top quark.

1995 Russian cosmonaut Valeri Polyakov completes a record 438-day mission on the space station Mir.

1994

1995

1994 A genetically modified tomato is marketed in the United States with the name "Flavr Savr."

1994 English mathematician Andrew Wiles offers a proof of Fermat's last theorem, a famous math problem posed over 300 years earlier.

1995 U.S. computer programmer James Gosling introduces the Java programming language.

Exploring Mars

Mars is the nearest planet to Earth. There are plans to send humans to the "red planet," but will such an expedition ever be possible?

Mars has always fascinated people. In 1610, Galileo Galilei was the first person to look at the planet through a telescope. In 1719, Mars was observed to have seasons, and it is the planet in our solar system that is most like Earth.

The first space probe to fly close to Mars and take photographs of its surface was *Mariner 4*, in 1965. The pictures revealed a barren, dusty red landscape, with no trace of life. Many other spacecraft have flown close to the planet since then. Machines have been landed on it in order to examine the surface more closely. In 2023, 18 spacecraft were in orbit around Mars,and five more were on the surface.

The barren red desert that covers much of Mars' surface.

TIMELINE
1995–1997

KEY:

- Biology and Medicine
- Engineering and Invention
- Astronomy and Math
- Chemistry and Physics

1995 U.S. geophysicists detect the rotation of Earth's solid inner core through analysis of seismic waves.

1995 The number of cars and trucks in the United States exceeds 200 million—more than one for every adult.

1996 European scientists produce the first example of antimatter, antihydrogen.

1996 U.S. astronomers find traces of what might be microscopic life in a meteorite that originated from Mars.

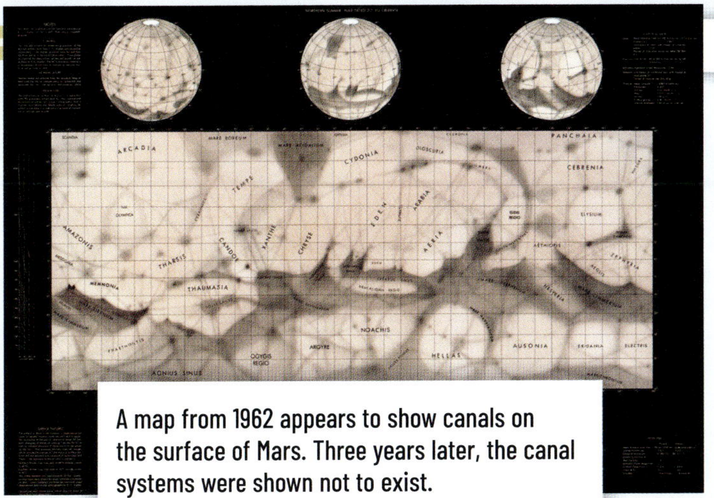

A map from 1962 appears to show canals on the surface of Mars. Three years later, the canal systems were shown not to exist.

Timeline

1719 Mars is observed to have seasons, similar to Earth

1877 Giovanni Schiaparelli claims to see "canal" on Mars

1965 The *Mariner 4* probe shows Mars is a barren planet

1997–2004 NASA lands three rovers on Mars: *Sojourner*, *Spirit*, and *Opportunity*

2012 *Curiosity* rover lands on Mars

2021 *Perseverance* rover lands on Mars carrying a small helicopter, *Ingenuity*

2023 NASA plans for a crewed flight to Mars in the 2030s

Rovers and Photography

The *Curiosity* rover landed in the Gale Crater on Mars in 2012. It was the fourth rover NASA had sent to the planet and was still operating in 2023. The *Curiosity* rover is the size of a car, and has been moving across the planet's surface, taking photographs and gathering rock samples.

NASA's *Perseverance* rover landed in the Jezero crater on Mars in 2021. *Perseverance* is also the size of a car, but it was better equipped. It carries seven instruments for examining samples, 19 cameras, and two microphones. In addition, *Perseverance* carried a small helicopter named *Ingenuity*. By 2023, *Ingenuity* had made 72

1996 DaimlerChrysler AG makes an experimental car that is powered by fuel cells.

1996 Scottish biologist Ian Wilmut clones a sheep named Dolly.

1997 U.S. physicists led by Eric Cornell produce an atomic laser.

1997 NASA probe *Mars Pathfinder* and its rover send back 16,500 images of the surface of Mars.

1997 U.S. geneticist Huntington Willard assembles an artificial human chromosome that successfully replicates.

1997 Long-period comet Hale-Bopp is a bright object in the night sky for several months as it passes close to Earth.

1996

1997

Canals on Mars?

In the 1860s, French astronomer Emmanuel Liais thought that the changes he observed on the surface of Mars through a telescope were due to changing seasonal vegetation. In 1877, Italian astronomer Giovanni Schiaparelli claimed there were seas and continents on the planet, and noted what he called "canali" (channels). His claim was taken up by a wealthy American Percival Lowell, who set up his own observatory and thought these channels were irrigation canals. Authors of fiction such as H. G. Wells wrote stories about there being intelligent life on the planet. All this speculation was shown to be valueless when the Mariner probes showed there was no life on the planet.

flights. Managing to achieve flight on a planet with a very thin atmosphere was quite a feat. So, too, was programming the helicopter so that it could control itself during takeoff and flight, because the distance from Earth meant that it was impossible to transmit effective instructions direct from NASA.

Mars rovers are all designed to examine the composition of the planet and its atmosphere, but more specifically they are searching for organic carbon or traces of microorganisms that might be evidence that there was once life on Mars. They are also searching for water. It is known that there is frozen water on Mars, but the planet's thin atmosphere means that liquid water immediately turns to water vapor. Water and oxygen are vital to support human exploration of the red planet, but it also has less than one percent of the amount of oxygen in Earth's atmosphere.

The *Curiosity* rover took this "selfie" of itself.

TIMELINE
1998–1999

KEY:

- Biology and Medicine
- Engineering and Invention
- Astronomy and Math
- Chemistry and Physics

1998 The world's largest passenger terminal opens at Chek Lap Kok Airport in Hong Kong.

1998 U.S. researchers grow human stem cells in the laboratory (stem cells may one day be used to treat cellular disorders).

1998

1998 Swiss scientists produce a titanium dioxide solar cell. It is twice as efficient as standard solar cells.

1998 After 15 years' work, an international project works out the genetic code for a whole animal—a tiny nematode worm.

Obstacles to Human Exploration

There are some major obstacles to be overcome before it will be possible to land humans on Mars. It would take a long time to get there and back—the minimum round trip would be about 21 months—and human body tissue does not respond well to such prolonged periods of weightlessness in space. Slowing a spacecraft down enough to land also has its problems in the thin Martian atmosphere, and another rocket would have to be carried for the return to Earth.

Added to these considerations are the dangers of being on the planet. Solar storms unleash radiation, which would make walking on the surface of Mars hazardous. The astronauts would also have to carry sufficient air to the planet. Using the Martian atmosphere might help—the crew could be breathing a mix of Martian argon and nitrogen, plus oxygen brought from Earth—but Mars' thin atmosphere is 95 percent carbon dioxide.

Despite these challenges, NASA eventually intends to send its Orion Multi-Purpose Crew Vehicle to Mars, with the astronauts carried in a Deep Space Habitat Module. Research is also being carried out in Europe. If the problems can be overcome, will Mars be the next space frontier?

The helicopter *Ingenuity* recorded 72 flights on Mars. It made its last flight in January 2024.

1999 Russia abandons its Mir space station after 13 years.

1999 A much-feared "millennium bug" fails to damage the world's computers on December 31.

1999

1999 According to the World Health Organization, AIDS becomes the main cause of death in Africa.

1999 Russian researchers create a new element, element 114.

Robots and Drones

Robots have become increasingly important during the 21st century. They can do jobs that are too dangerous or boring for people to do.

The word "robot" was first used in the 1920s by a Czech author. The term comes from the Czech word "robota," meaning "work." In the ancient world people had various machines that appeared to work on their own. These "automata" were operated by levers and pulleys. Since then, many inventors dreamed of creating machines that could perform manual work. However, it was not until electricity became widely available in the 20th century that robots were created. Before then, the sources needed to power

Robots at work on the production line of a modern electronics factory. They are able to carry out very precise repetitive actions.

TIMELINE
2000–2001

KEY:

Biology and Medicine

Engineering and Invention

Astronomy and Math

2000 Scientists on the Human Genome Project produce a rough draft of the sequence of the human genome.

2000 Geneticists figure out the complete genome sequence of the fruit fly *Drosophila*.

2000

2000 NASA's space probe *Galileo* reveals that Io, one of Jupiter's moons, is highly volcanic.

2000 British inventor Matthew Allwork perfects a gyrostabilized camera that runs along tracks to televise sports events.

An agricultural robot on a "smart farm" selecting and picking plants that are ready for market .

them, such as steam engines, were large and heavy. As electrical components became smaller and more efficient, so machines were able to take on more autonomous functions. With advances in computer science in the late 20th century, computer programs became more complex, and the hardware for robots was smaller. The great step forward came in the 21st century, when further advances in computer sciences meant that robots were able to process information from their environment and react to changing situations.

Timeline

1903 Spanish inventor Leonardo Torres Quevedo creates a radio-based control system for machines

1921 The term "robot" is used in a play by Czech science fiction author Karel Čapek

1961 First programmable industrial robot, "Unimate," is patented

1991 John R. Adler's Cyberknife radiosurgical system is installed at Stanford University

1997 *Sojourner* robot vehicle explores Mars; it avoids obstacles without human direction

2002 Roomba, a robot vacuum cleaner, is launched

2014 Tesla launches driverless cars

2001 Surgeons in New York City use computers to operate on a woman in France.

2001 Gray wolves are found living wild in Germany, 150 years after they were thought to have died out in the wild.

2001

2001 A NASA probe lands on the surface of the asteroid Eros.

2001 The Very Large Telescope (VLT) is completed at the Paranal Observatory in Chile.

Robot Takeover!

Many works of fiction warn of the dangers of robots, such as the film *The Terminator* or the Robot series of books written by Isaac Asimov, in which three rules have to be programmed into robots to keep them under control. Such stories suggest that robots could develop into superior beings and take over the world. But the real danger comes from the humans who create and program the robots in the first place. In the real world robots do not possess human aggression or desire for power.

Arnold Schwarzenegger in *The Terminator* (1984), a film that plays on fears about robots.

Making Decisions

Some people fear robots because they think they are artificial humans and the stuff of science fiction. However, robots are simply machines that undertake tasks. A domestic appliance such as a washing machine is a kind of robot. It takes care of the work that would once have been performed by one or more people.

Robots work in three main ways. They may be preprogrammed to undertake a certain set of tasks, as with robots building cars on an assembly line in a factory. They may be directly controlled by a human operator; for example, artificial hands directed by human operators are used to pick up hot or radioactive material in situations where it would be too dangerous for humans to do the job. Finally, they may be driven by computer programs of such complexity that the robots appear to be making their own decisions. An example of this would be the vacuum cleaner that can

TIMELINE
2002–2004

KEY:
- Biology and Medicine
- Engineering and Invention
- Astronomy and Math
- Chemistry and Physics

2002 The Hubble Space Telescope is upgraded by a NASA mission.

2002 U.S. chemists synthesize a compound of uranium and the rare gas neon.

2002

2002 Researchers in Texas clone a domestic cat.

2002 Researchers at the University of New York produce a synthetic virus.

A military drone, partly controlled by an operator but programmed to destroy a specific target or perform reconnaissance tasks.

move around a house cleaning the floors without bumping into anything. Robots are now used every day in domestic and industrial situations, and usually without us even noticing them.

Military Drones and Robots

One area where robots have become particularly important is in warfare. During the 1970s, toward the end of the Vietnam War, so-called "smart" weapons were introduced. These large glide bombs, remotely operated by a pilot, automatically tracked targets. Since then, unpiloted combat aerial vehicles (UCAVs) have been used for reconnaissance, surveillance, and attack. The operator controls the drone from a remote location. During the war in Ukraine that began in February 2022, drones were effective weapons against heavily armored tanks.

2003 NASA's space shuttle *Columbia is destroyed* as it reenters Earth's atmosphere, killing all of the crew.

2003 An outbreak of severe acute respiratory syndrome (SARS) in Asia spreads worldwide.

2003 Austrian Felix Baumgartner "skyglides" across the English Channel in a special suit.

2004 U.S. physicists announce a helium-based "supersolid" that flows through another material without friction.

2004 Medical researchers in South Korea clone human embryos to obtain stem cells for therapeutic purposes.

COVID-19

Early in 2020, physicians became aware that a deadly new virus was spreading across the world. It quickly became a pandemic.

The infection named COVID-19 is caused by the coronavirus SARS-CoV-2 (SARS stands for severe acute respiratory syndrome). Cases of the disease were first identified in China in late 2019. The disease most likely originated in bats, as a mutation from a coronavirus they already carried. It seems to have been transmitted to other wild animals, and through them to humans in a food market in the city of Wuhan. There were theories that the virus came from a Chinese government laboratory, but the World Health Organization does not support this.

COVID-19 then spread rapidly, the virus being transmitted between humans via particles breathed out by an infected person. The virus particles enter the nose, mouth, or eyes and then

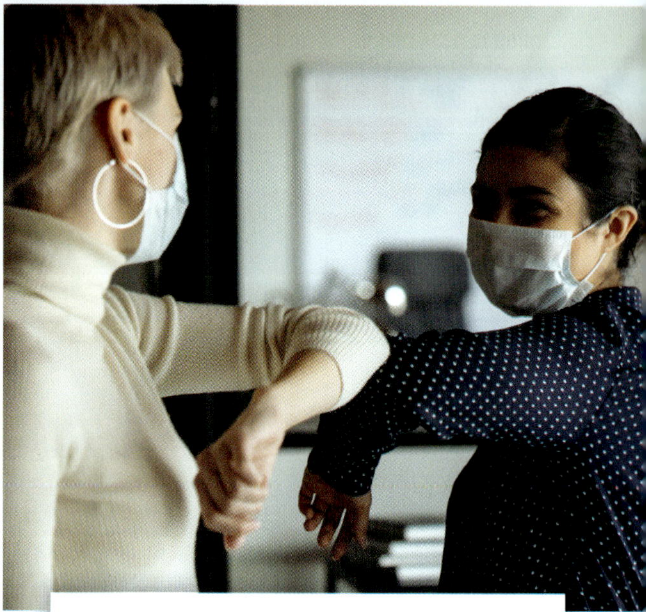

Wearing masks and making sure there was minimal contact with other people's hands became routine during the COVID-19 pandemic.

TIMELINE
2004-2006

KEY:

Biology and Medicine

Engineering and Invention

Astronomy and Math

Chemistry and Physics

2004 Paleontologists on Flores Island, Indonesia, discover the remains of a 3-feet (90-cm) tall hominid, *Homo floresiensis.*

2005 A projectile fired from a NASA probe collides with Comet Tempel 1, allowing scientists to study the plume of icy debris thrown up by the impact.

2005 U.S. geophysicists discover that lightning flashes produce bursts of X-rays.

Cleaning tables in a restaurant with anti-viral spray. COVID-19 was easily transmitted through touching infected surfaces.

multiply in the lungs. These particles are airborne, and if they land on a surface and a person touches it, particles can stick to their hands. The person becomes infected if they touch their mouth or rub their eyes.

Worldwide Pandemic

People are infectious, meaning they can pass on the disease, even before they show any symptoms. Some people, perhaps over 40 percent, never show any symptoms but can still pass on the disease. The disease spread quickly, and at the beginning of the pandemic the number of people affected was rising every day. The virus reached Italy on January 31, 2020, via tourists from China. Within weeks the hospitals and emergency services in northern Italy were almost overwhelmed. It then spread rapidly worldwide.

Timeline

December 2019 The first cases of COVID-19 appear in Wuhan, China

February 2020 The World Health Organization calls the new disease COVID-19 or SARS-CoV-2

19 March 2020 Italy suffers the most COVID-related fatalities per week

August 2020 The Oxford-AstraZeneca vaccine enters Phase III testing

December 2020 Some vaccines approved and go into mass production

2021 The Omicron variant of COVID-19 becomes dominant in the U.S.

December 2023 Over 13 billion doses of vaccines have been administered worldwide

2005 The Genographic Project is set up to map the history of human migration through DNA.

2005 NASA's shuttle fleet is grounded indefinitely after problems with heat-shield tiles on *Discovery*.

2005

2006

2006 Scientists in Canada discover the fossil of a "missing link" between fish and four-legged vertebrates.

2006 NASA launches the probe *New Horizons* on a nine-year voyage to Pluto.

2006 Boeing launches the world's largest airplane, the 747 Large Cargo Freighter (known as the Dreamlifter).

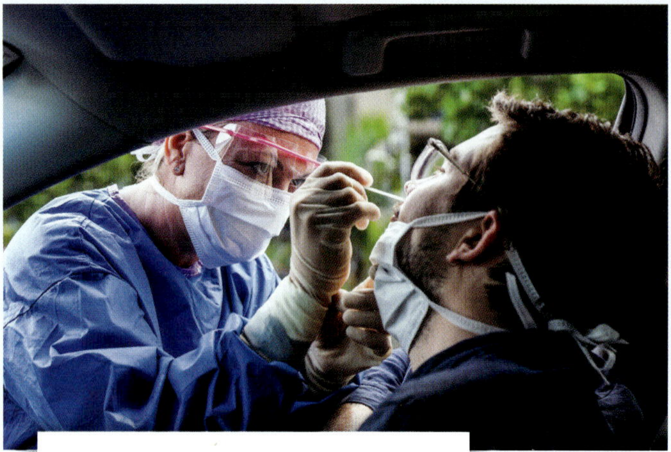

Testing for COVID-19 became widespread, and often involved drive-through centers. Here, a physician takes a nasal swab.

By the end of March 2020, the highest number of confirmed cases in the world were recorded in the United States of America.

Vulnerability

The COVID virus attacks the respiratory system, and is particularly dangerous for older people and anyone with an existing respiratory disease. Research figures indicate that a 25-year-old with COVID-19 has only a 0.01 percent chance of dying, but an 85-year-old has a 15 percent chance of dying. In countries with an older population, such as Italy, 2 percent of people who caught COVID died. For those with mild infections, the symptoms of shortness of breath, fatigue, and fever usually last between one to two weeks. Severe cases can last for months. In so-called "long COVID," sufferers (estimated to be between 10 and 30 percent of infected people) experience symptoms that weaken them over many months or even years.

With numbers of cases rising at an alarming rate, governments took action to keep people isolated from each other. In some cases personal contact between different households was forbidden in order to reduce the likelihood of transmission. Nations went into lockdown. Other

TIMELINE
2007–2009

KEY:

Biology and Medicine

Engineering and Invention

Astronomy and Math

Chemistry and Physics

2007 Scientists in Massachusetts power a light bulb with "wireless" electricity.

2007 Geneticist J. Craig Venter publishes his entire genetic sequence, the first of a single person.

2007

2007 U.S. company Apple markets the iPhone, a multimedia smartphone with a touch screen.

2007 Scientists in Scotland develop a genetically modified chicken whose eggs contain anticancer proteins.

preventative measures, such as wearing masks and gloves, were introduced. There was intense debate about these policies.

The good news for the world was that scientists had been on the alert for such an infectious disease for decades. The Ebola virus, MERS (Middle East Respiratory Syndrome), and other potential killers had already been extensively researched. The breakthrough with COVID came with the use of strategies that had been developed to combat MERS. The two most effective techniques were vaccines that used RNA or messenger RNA, and ones that were viral vector vaccines with an adenovirus shell containing DNA.

It is estimated that over 15 million lives were saved by the vaccination of large populations. COVID-19 went through several variants, but vaccines were developed to target these variants. Although COVID-19 has not gone away, the fight to control it has been a success.

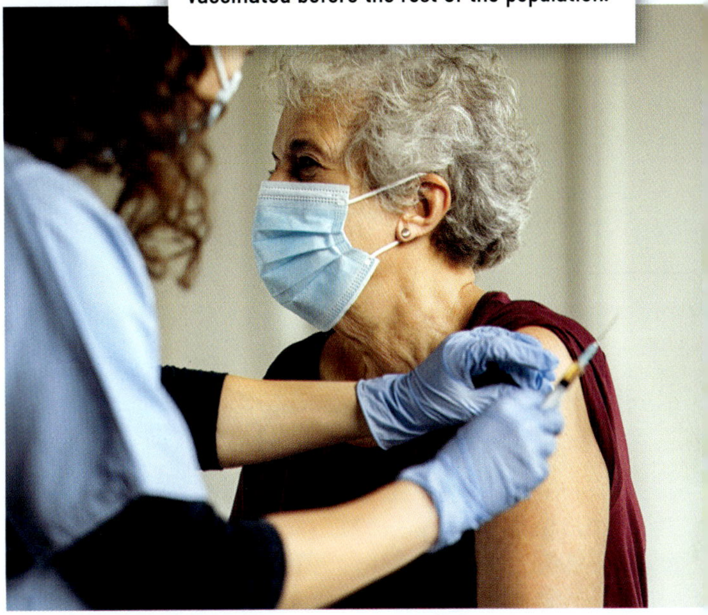

A woman is vaccinated against the disease. Senior citizens were among the most vulnerable, and were generally vaccinated before the rest of the population.

2008 India launches its first lunar spacecraft.

2008 The Large Hadron Collider is switched on at the European Organization for Nuclear Research (CERN). Nine days later, it is switched off again because of a fault.

2008 Researchers in England produce human-cow embryos, which they hope will provide stem cells to develop therapies for human disorders.

2009 Japanese scientists report that decomposing plastics are creating a "toxic soup" in the oceans.

2009 The Human Genome Organization reports that DNA studies suggest Asia was populated in a single migration from the south.

Artificial Intelligence

Intelligent machines, once the subject of science fiction, seem to have become reality. Computers can now play chess at the highest level, or write verse in the style of Shakespeare.

The basics of artificial intelligence have been part of the science of computing since the 1950s. Computer pioneer Alan Turing used the term "machine intelligence," and "artificial intelligence" was coined after his death in 1954. As early as 1951, scientists created programs for playing checkers and chess. Over the next six decades, there were constant refinements in the capabilities of computers. They can search through swathes of data and make mathematical calculations quickly. Researchers then looked at ways in which computers could be made to solve problems. One method was to program the typical human "rule of thumb" for dealing with certain problems; another was a "local search" method, whereby the computer always looks for an answer that will aid its quest. For example, moving up a hill by taking steps that lead upward, not downward. In addition,

Alan Turing, the scientist who first wrote about the possibility of machine intelligence.

TIMELINE
2010–2020

KEY:
- Biology and Medicine
- Engineering and Invention
- Astronomy and Math

2010 Apple launches the iPad, a tablet computer operated by a touch screen.

2011 The first 4-terabyte hard drive for a computer goes on sale.

2012 *Curiosity* rover lands on Mars. It was still operating in 2023.

2013 An extinct species, the gastric brooding frog, is cloned in Australia using preserved tissue.

ChatGPT (Chat Generative Pre-trained Transformer) became popular after its launch in November 2022. ChatGPT is based on a large language model. It can even write music in different styles.

programmers added some aspects of probability theory drawn from economics. The idea was to make computers produce answers even though the basic data was not entirely clear. The computer could try various approaches to a problem and decide on the best result. Decades of research and experimentation went into this.

Chess Champions

Computers were able to master some complex but limited fields, such as board games. Deep Blue beat world chess champion Gary Kasparov in 1997, and AlphaGo beat reigning Go world champion Ke Jei in 2017. Meanwhile, researchers had been working hard to refine computer command of language, and to make

Timeline

1951 Alan Turing writes the paper "Computing Machinery and Intelligence"

1994 A graphics processing unit is incorporated in the PlayStation gaming console

1997 Deep Blue chess computer defeats world champion Gary Kasparov

2009 Fei-Fei Li presents the ImageNet idea at a conference in Florida

2017 One in five U.S. companies claim to use AI in some form

2021 AlphaFold 2 replicates the structure of a protein in a matter of hours

2023 A global summit is held to discuss the risks of AI and how to control it

2016 2017 2018 2020

2016 An artificial pancreas that can regulate insulin levels in the human body is created.

2017 The computer AlphaGo beats reigning world champion Ke Jei at the board game Go.

2018 In Rome, Italian scientists demonstrate a bionic hand that has a sense of touch and can operate independently of laboratory control.

2020 COVID-19 sweeps the world. By August, effective vaccines are being trialed.

A scientist examines human tissue under a microscope. AI has proven better at diagnosis than physicians in some areas of medicine.

computers identify images. From 2012, there were two new developments. The first was an increase in the power and speed of computers due to the use of graphics processing units (GPU). These had originally been developed for computer games in the 1990s. The second was the availability of more data than ever before on the internet. This data could be stored by the huge memory banks of new programs. Some of this was part of free information sites such as Wikipedia. A major boost was given by the existence of ImageNet, which became a huge digital image database that stored 14 million images by the early 2020s.

Deep Learning

The result of these advances was that computer scientists were able to construct programs that used "deep learning." These programs have various layers of information. For example, one layer of a program might

TIMELINE
2021–2024

KEY:

Biology and Medicine

Engineering and Invention

Astronomy and Math

2021

2021 *Perseverance* rover lands on Mars. It carries a small helicopter that makes 72 flights.

2021 The Tesla Model 3 becomes the first electric car to sell a million units.

2022

2022 The complete human genome is accurately sequenced.

2022 The AI program ChatGPT is released. It provokes fears about artificial intelligence.

work out the colors in a painting. Another level might be able to compare the painting to other works of art produced in the same period. However, the interesting thing about deep learning is that computer programs seem to be able to improve their performance as they get feedback about what works and what does not work.

Good or Bad?

Computer programs now have the ability to write articles, assemble advertising posters, or write music. A major benefit is in medical diagnosis, where a computer can often sift through many more diagnostic possibilities than a single physician. There are, however, potential drawbacks to AI. One might be the loss of human jobs to AI machines. Another is that AI could steal a person's copyright—using their style of speaking or writing, or creating fake images. More immediately concerning, perhaps, are the uses that unscrupulous individuals, governments, or groups could put AI to. Some states already use face recognition to control their citizens. In the early 2020s, many countries began setting up legal frameworks to control AI.

One of the potential dangers of AI is that surveillance cameras feed into AI programs to give repressive governments detailed information about their citizens.

2023 The Nobel Prize in Medicine is awarded to Katalin Karakó and Drew Weissman for their work on an mRNA vaccine to combat COVID-19.

2023 The UN Climate Change Conference decides that current action by governments is too limited to combat climate change.

2023

2024

2024 U.S. company Intuitive Machines puts a lander, *Odysseus*, on the moon. It is the first moon landing by a commercial company.

2024 The Japanese space agency lands a probe, *Smart Lander*, on the moon.

Glossary

atom The smallest unit into which matter can be divided and still retain its chemical identity.

chromosome A threadlike structure in the nucleus of a living cell that carries genetic information.

DNA (deoxyribonucleic acid) A chemical substance that, with proteins, makes up the chromosomes found in the nuclei of most cells; the basis of genetic inheritance in most living organisms.

electron A negatively charged subatomic particle.

gene The basic unit of inheritance that influences a characteristic of a living organism.

ion An atom or molecule that has acquired an electrical charge.

laser (light amplification by stimulated emission of radiation) A device that produces an intense beam of light that is monochromatic (all of the same wavelength) and coherent (all the light waves are synchronized).

nucleotide A basic unit of packaging of DNA in a chromosome, in which a sugar molecule is linked to one or more phosphate groups.

nucleus, atomic (pl nuclei) The positively charged dense region at the center of an atom, composed of protons and neutrons.

neutron A subatomic particle that has no electrical charge and is found in the atomic nucleus.

pandemic A disease event in which there are more cases of a disease than expected, spread over several countries or continents, usually involving person-to-person transmission and affecting a very large number of people.

payload The part of a cargo that earns revenue.

proton A positively charged subatomic particle in the atomic nucleus.

radioactivity The emission of particles or radiation by atomic nuclei.

RNA (ribonucleic acid) A molecule present in most living organisms and viruses. Made up of nucleotides, ribose sugars attached to nitrogenous bases and phosphate groups.

subatomic particle Any particle that is smaller than an atom.

superconductor A substance that shows no resistance to the passage of electrical current (usually at very low temperatures).

synthesize To chemically form a compound from simpler elements.

vaccine A preparation containing viruses or other microorganisms introduced into the body to stimulate antibodies to build up immunity against infectious disease.

Further Information

Books

Borus, Audrey. *James Watson, Francis Crick, Rosalind Franklin, and Maurice Wilkins. The Scientists Who Revealed the Structure of DNA.* Rosen Publishing, 2021.

Gordon, Sherri Mabry. *Internet Security and You* (The Promise and Perils of Technology). Rosen Publishing 2020.

Louriero, Stephanie. *Fossil Fuels: A Graphic Guide* (The Climate Crisis). Lerner Publishing Group, 2024.

Lucas, Eileen. *Charles Babbage and Ada Lovelace. The Pen Pals Who Imagined the First Computer* (Scientific Collaboration). Rosen Publishing, 2021.

Phillips, Howard. *Inside DNA and RNA (Inside Modern Genetics).* Rosen Publishing 2022.

Starr, Abbe Lynn. *Explore Robotics* (Searchlight Books: High-Tech Science). Lerner Publishing Group, 2024.

Websites

www.computersciencelab.com/ComputerHistory/History.htm
An illustrated history of computers.

www.genome.gov/genetics-glossary/Deoxyribonucleic-Acid#:~:text=Deoxyribonucleic%20acid%20(abbreviated%20DNA)%20is,known%20as%20a%20double%20helix.
An explanation of DNA, with links and narration.

www.ibm.com/topics/artificial-intelligence
Introduction to all aspects of artificial intelligence, including a timeline history and explanations of its uses and developments.

www.nasa.gov/the-apollo-program/
NASA history of the Apollo program.

www.mars.nasa.gov/
NASA pages on Mars exploration.

robotsguide.com/learn/types-of-robots
All about the different types of robots and drones, along with photographs and links.

Publisher's note to educators and parents: Our editors have carefully reviewed these websites to ensure that they are suitable for students. Many websites change frequently, however, and we cannot guarantee that a site's future contents will continue to meet our high standards of quality and educational value. Be advised that students should be closely supervised whenever they access the internet.

Index